Functional Skills

ICT

Entry Level 3, Level 1 and Level 2

This book is for anyone doing Entry Level 3, Level 1 or Level 2 Functional Skills ICT. It covers everything you need, whichever exam board you're studying.

All the topics are explained in a straightforward way, with test-style tasks to give you plenty of realistic practice before the final test.

Since 1995, CGP study books have helped millions of students do well in their tests and exams. We cover dozens of subjects for all ages — and we always keep our prices as low as possible.

Study & Test P...

Contents

Section Five — Spreadsheets

Section Six — Charts and Graphs

Section Seven — Presentations

Section Eight — Databases

Test-style Tasks

Published by CGP

Editors:
Katie Braid, Jane Ellingham, Rob Harrison, Gordon Henderson,
Christopher Lindle, Lyn Setchel and Dawn Wright.

With thanks to Andy Bennington, Nicola Bowman, Charlotte Burrows, Neil Hastings,
Simon Little, David Norden and Glenn Rogers for the proofreading and reviewing.

ISBN: 978 1 78294 142 2

With thanks to Jan Greenway for the copyright research.

Groovy website: www.cgpbooks.co.uk

Printed by Elanders Ltd, Newcastle upon Tyne.
Jolly bits of clipart from CorelDRAW®

How to Use this Book

Layout of the Book

1) This book is split up into **eight main sections** covering all the **Functional Skills criteria for ICT**.

2) Each section contains the main content with **screen shots** and **examples** to explain how to use the **features** of certain programs.

3) There will also be **Practice Tasks** to complete — these allow you to **practise** using the features explained in the main content.

4) You can just dip in and out of this book. But it is more sensible to **work through** each section **in order** — this will help you build up your skills.

5) At the end of the book there is also a **Test-style Tasks** section.

6) This provides **separate**, exam-like practice for Entry Level 3, Level 1 and Level 2.

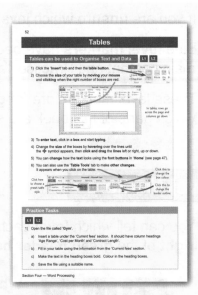

Task Files and Answer Files

1) For most of the Practice Tasks, and for the Test-style Tasks section, you'll need access to task files and answer files.

2) These task files and answer files can be **downloaded** from our website:

www.cgpbooks.co.uk/fsict

3) When you click on a link to a file you'll be asked what you want to do with it — you need to save it on your computer where you will be able to find it again. For example, choose '**Save as**', select where you'd like to save it, then press '**Save**'.

4) The file will be saved as a **compressed (zipped)** file — explained more on page 20.

5) Tutors can download this material for their students and store it in a suitable place.

Microsoft® Windows® 7 and Office® 2010

1) This book was written using **Microsoft® Windows® 7** and **Office® 2010**.

2) If you are using a **different version** of Windows® or Office® then you can still use this book, but the **features** may look **different**.

3) Also, the task files and answer files may look or behave slightly **differently**.

4) The features and files will be **quite different** if you are using **non-Microsoft software**.

Levels and Exam Boards

1) This book is for anyone studying **Entry Level 3**, **Level 1** or **Level 2** Functional Skills ICT with **any exam board**.

2) If you are **unsure** which level or exam board you are studying, **ask your tutor**.

3) Blue **level markers** have been used to **show** what **level** the main content and Practice Tasks are suitable for (see below).

EL3   L1   L2

4) These level markers are for **guidance only** — you should **check** with your **tutor** which parts of this book are **suitable** for **your level and exam board**.

Level Markers

1) You can tell which **level** each box is for by looking at the **blue level markers** to the **right** of the **green header boxes**:

EL3   L1   L2   When all three markers are there, that box is for Entry Level 3, Level 1 and Level 2.

L1   L2   When just the L1 and L2 markers are there, that box is for Level 1 and Level 2 only.

L2   When just the L2 box is there, that box is for Level 2 only.

For example, the box below is for Entry level 3, Level 1 and Level 2:

Choosing a Website   EL3   L1   L2

1) Anyone can put **anything** on the internet.

2) So you need to use **websites** you can **trust**.

3) Here are some things to **look for**:

2) The **same** three blue markers are used to show the **levels** for each **Practice Task** too. But here they're found just **above each task**.
For example, the task below is for Entry Level 3, Level 1 and Level 2 students:

Practice Tasks

EL3   L1   L2

1) Open the file called '**Gino**'.

a) Write your name in cell A1.

b) Go to cell C5 and change £2.75 to £2.00.

Getting Started

Basic Computer Parts `EL3` `L1` `L2`

1) Computers **don't** always look the same.

2) But most **desktop personal computers (PCs)** will look similar to this:

Computer unit or case — contains all the pieces that make the computer work. You put disks in here and also plug other things in here.

Keyboard — has keys with letters, numbers and symbols, which you press to enter information (see p. 5).

Monitor (screen) — what you're working on is displayed on it.

Printer — used to make paper copies of files on your computer (like letters or spreadsheets).

Mouse — used to move a pointer around the screen and click on things (see p. 5).

3) **Don't worry** about breaking a computer just by using it — that's pretty **difficult** to do.

Computers Come in Different Sizes `EL3` `L1` `L2`

1) **Laptops** (or **notebooks**) —
These are small computers that can be **folded up**. This means they are easy to **carry** around and take up **less space** than desktop computers.

2) **Netbooks** —
These are like laptops but **smaller** and a bit **less powerful**.

3) **Tablets** —
These are **hand-held** computers that come in different sizes but are **smaller** than laptops. They often have **touchscreens** instead of a keyboard. Some are specially made to read electronic versions of books, these are called **e-readers**.

4) **Smartphones** —
These are **mobile phones** that work like computers. You can install programs on them called **apps** which can do all sorts of things. They often have a **touchscreen**.

5) **Other machines** —
Lots of other things you use everyday have computers **inside them** too.
For example, microwaves, washing machines, cars, cash machines...

Computers are Made of Hardware and Software   EL3 L1 L2

1) **Hardware** is all the **physical parts** of a computer — not just the obvious parts like the monitor, keyboard and printer, but also all the bits inside that make it work.

2) **Software** is all the **programs** in a computer that make it do different things — they contain instructions that tell the computer what to do. Computers use **two kinds** of software — an **operating system** and **application software** (see p. 9 for more).

Starting Up and Shutting Down   EL3 L1 L2

1) To start, push the **power button** on the **computer unit**.

2) You need to press the **power button** on the **monitor** too.

3) Sometimes you'll need to **log on** before you can use the computer (see below).

4) To **shut down** a computer, find the '**Start**' button first. It's often in the **bottom left** of the screen. If you're using Microsoft® Windows® 7 it will look like this.

5) Press the '**Start**' button, then click '**Shut down**'.

6) Always switch off a computer **properly**. Just switching off using the **power button** or the **plug** might mean that you **lose or damage data**.

Power buttons will often have this symbol on them: ⏻

Logging On and Off   EL3 L1 L2

1) Some computers are used by **lots of different people**.

2) Each user will need to **log on** when they want to use it.

3) When you **start up** the computer, **instructions** will appear telling you how to log on.

4) You'll usually need to press '**Ctrl**', '**Alt**' and '**Delete**' at the same time.

5) This will bring up a window where you can enter your **username** and **password**, then press '**Return**' or the arrow button on the log on window.

6) Usernames and passwords need to be **spelt correctly** and include any **capitals**, so **type** them in **carefully**. (See p. 7 for more on passwords.)

7) To log off, click the '**Start**' button and click the **arrow button** next to the 'Shut down' button. Then select '**Log off**' from the menu that pops up.

8) Log off leaves the computer **on**, but someone else can log on. Use '**Shut down**' to switch off the computer properly (see above).

Typing and the Keyboard   EL3   L1   L2

1) Use the keyboard to **enter text** into a computer:

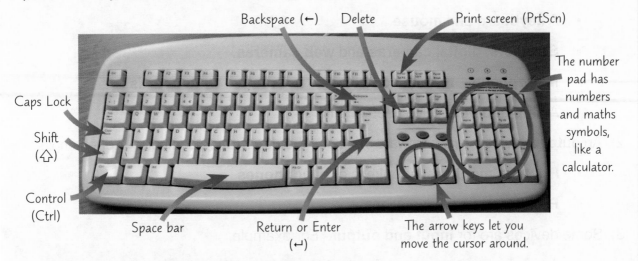

Backspace (←)   Delete   Print screen (PrtScn)

Caps Lock

Shift
(⇧)

Control
(Ctrl)

Space bar

Return or Enter
(↵)

The arrow keys let you move the cursor around.

The number pad has numbers and maths symbols, like a calculator.

2) Press '**Enter**' or '**Return**' to move to a **new line**.

3) Use the '**Space bar**' to make spaces **between words** and **after commas** and **full stops**.

4) Hold down '**Shift**' whilst typing to get **capital letters**.

5) Press '**Caps Lock**' once to write **everything** in **capitals**. Press it again to **turn it off**.

6) If a key has **two symbols** on it, hold '**Shift**' and press the key to get the **top symbol**.

7) Press '**Delete**' or '**Backspace**' to **remove characters**. 'Backspace' deletes the character to the **left** of the cursor, 'Delete' removes the one to the **right** of the cursor.

8) Press '**Print Screen**' to **capture** an **image** of what's **on the screen**.

Use the Mouse to Control the Pointer   EL3   L1   L2

1) The **pointer** or **cursor** is the **symbol** which you use to **control a computer**.

2) The pointer is seen on the **screen**, often as an **arrow** or a **line** like this: I

3) As you **move** the **mouse**, the pointer will **move too**.

4) The mouse has **buttons** which you can **click** to do things **on the screen**.

Left button

Right button

5) You will mostly use the **left mouse button**. In this book, if it says to '**click**' something it means **move** your **pointer** onto it and click the **left mouse** button **once**.

6) If you need to use your **right mouse button** it will say '**right-click**'.

7) A '**double-click**' means pressing the **left** button **twice very quickly**.

Input and Output Devices   EL3   L1   L2

1) An **input device** is any hardware used to **enter data** into a computer. For example:

   - A **keyboard** and **mouse**.

   - **Scanners**, **digital cameras** and **web cameras**.

   - **Microphones**, **remote controls** and **interactive whiteboards**.

   - A **chip and pin** device used at a till.

2) An **output device** is any hardware that **uses** the **data from** a computer. For example:

   - **Printers**, **monitors**, **speakers** or **headphones**.

   - **Projectors** for presentations.

3) Some devices are for **input and output**. For example:

   - A **touchscreen** on a **mobile phone** or **self-service checkout**.

   - A **headset** which includes a **microphone** and a **speaker**.

Practice Tasks

EL3   L1   L2

1) a)   Start up your computer. Log on if required.

   b)   Shut down your computer properly.

EL3   L1   L2

2) Why is it important to shut down a computer properly?

   ....

   ....

EL3   L1   L2

3) Which button would you press on the keyboard if you wanted
   to capture an image of what was on the computer screen?

   ....

EL3   L1   L2

4) Name one input device, one output device and one device which is both.

   ....

   ....

Security — Passwords and Viruses

Passwords Protect Your Information EL3 L1 L2

1) Passwords **stop** other people from **logging on** to your computer (see page 4).

2) Passwords can also be used to stop people from **reading** your **private information** or **messing around** with your **work**.

3) For example, **documents (files)** and **USB memory sticks** can be password-protected, you can use a password to lock your **mobile phone**, and even your **bank card PIN** is a type of password.

4) Passwords are **only good** if you choose them **carefully** though.

5) **Don't** have a password that's **easy** for other people to **guess**. This means you should **avoid** things like your name, date of birth, pet's name, favourite team...

6) A **good** password contains a **mixture** of **letters** and **numbers**, maybe some **capital** letters, and even **symbols** if allowed (for example, ! or *).

7) If you need to **write down** your password to remember it, keep it in a **safe place**.

8) Remember to **type** passwords in **carefully** when they're needed.

Opening a Password-Protected Document EL3 L1 L2

When you try to **open** a **password-protected document** (or file) a **window** or **box** will usually appear and ask you to **enter** the password. For example:

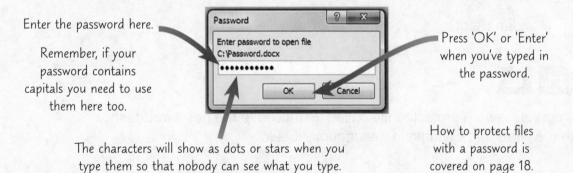

Enter the password here.

Remember, if your password contains capitals you need to use them here too.

Press 'OK' or 'Enter' when you've typed in the password.

The characters will show as dots or stars when you type them so that nobody can see what you type.

How to protect files with a password is covered on page 18.

Viruses Can Harm Your Computer EL3 L1 L2

1) A computer **virus** is a **harmful** program made to **infect** computers.

2) They can make things **stop working**, make the computer **run slower** or **steal** information from the computer.

3) Viruses can enter a computer through **files**, **emails** and the **internet**.

How to Avoid Viruses   EL3 L1 L2

1) The best way to **reduce** the risk of **viruses** is to use **antivirus software**.

2) This can **stop** viruses **entering** and **get rid** of viruses that are on a computer.

3) It's important to use **up-to-date** antivirus software and **run** a
   scan **frequently** to make sure your computer is kept safe.

4) You should also be careful **not to open** any **files** or
   email **attachments**, or **download** anything from
   the **internet** unless you know that they're **safe**.

   Email attachments are files that are sent with emails see page 35.

5) You can also run a virus **scan** on files **before** you **open** them.
   Then you can **remove them** from your computer if they're infected.

Practice Tasks

EL3 L1 L2

1) Jane works at CGP Books. She's an Aries and her date of birth is 18th April 1980.
   Her pet dog is called Snuffles and she drives a red Mini.
   Which of the passwords shown below would be a good password? Tick one box.

   ☐ JaneEllingham

   ☐ Enaj2675Boo

   ☐ CGPBooks123

   ☐ JaneApril

EL3 L1 L2

See page 14 for more on opening files.

2) Open the password protected file called '**Fruit**'. Use the password tasty.
   Write the word that's written in the document below.

   ....

EL3 L1 L2

3) Describe one way you can protect your computer from viruses.

   ....

   ....

Software (Programs)

What is Software? EL3 L1 L2

1) Software means the **programs** that a computer **runs**.

2) They are sets of **instructions** that make all the bits of **hardware** work together.

3) Computers use **two different** kinds of software
— an **operating system** (OS) and **application software**.

4) An OS is the software that controls the whole computer system.
Some examples are Windows®, UNIX®, Mac OS® X.
The OS runs the application software...

5) The **application software** are the programs like word processors, spreadsheet programs, email programs, database programs, internet browsers...

In this book, when we say software or program we mean application software.

Types of Application Software EL3 L1 L2

There are lots of **different types of software**. Here are some important ones:

Type of Software	What it Does	Examples
Internet Browser	Lets you look at web pages and download material from the internet.	Internet Explorer®, Mozilla Firefox®, Google™ Chrome™.
Email	Allows you to send electronic messages and files from one computer to another or lots of others.	Microsoft® Outlook®, Gmail™, Mozilla® Thunderbird®.
Word Processor	Lets you create documents (files) with text and graphics, like letters, leaflets, posters and flyers.	Microsoft® Word®, Corel™ WordPerfect®.
Spreadsheet	Allows you to store and organise a lot of data (usually numbers). It can be used to carry out calculations and create charts using the data.	Microsoft® Excel®, LibreOffice™ Calc.
Database	Lets you store and organise a large amount of data. You can search the data quickly and produce reports.	Microsoft® Access®, LibreOffice™ Base.
Presentation	Lets you create slide shows or handouts for using in talks and presentations.	Microsoft® PowerPoint®, OpenOffice™ Impress.

Choosing the Right Software for the Job   EL3 L1 L2

1) It's important to be able to **pick the right software** for the **task** you need to complete.

2) In the **test**, you might have to **decide yourself** which type of **software** to use.

3) Make sure you **know** what each type of software **can do**.

4) This table lists some **tasks** and the best type of **software** to use:

Task	Software to use
Searching for information or images on the internet.	Internet Browser
Sending email messages and attachments.	Email
Producing files with text and graphics, like letters, leaflets, posters, newsletters, and flyers, etc.	Word Processor
Organising number data and carrying out calculations.	Spreadsheet
Producing a chart or graph from number data.	Spreadsheet
Organising data, running queries and producing reports.	Database
Producing slides or handouts for a talk.	Presentation

Practice Tasks

EL3 L1 L2

1) You are given some number data and asked to carry out some calculations with it. Which type of software should you use?

....

EL3 L1 L2

2) Name one task which presentation software would be useful for.

....

EL3 L1 L2

3) Jane has been asked to produce a document advertising the local bird watching club. It'll contain text and photos all about birds. Suggest which type of software Jane should use.

....

Windows, Icons and Buttons

The User Interface   EL3 L1 L2

1) A **user interface** is the technical term for the way the user (you) **communicates** with the computer.

2) **Different** types of **software** will have interfaces that **look** and **work differently**.

3) They usually always have **windows**, **icons**, **buttons**, **menus** and a **pointer** though:

This is a **window** (or box). In this one you can see what's inside a folder.

This is a **toolbar**. It has useful **buttons** on it.

This **minimises** the window.

This **maximises** the window (so it fills the whole screen).

This is the **pointer** (see p. 5)

This 'X' button will close the window if you click it.

This is a **menu**. It has different options which can be clicked on.

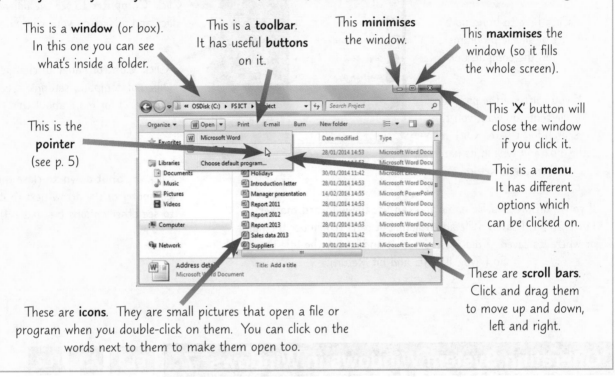

These are **scroll bars**. Click and drag them to move up and down, left and right.

These are **icons**. They are small pictures that open a file or program when you double-click on them. You can click on the words next to them to make them open too.

The Main Work Area is the Desktop   EL3 L1 L2

The **desktop** is usually what you'll see after you've **logged onto** your **computer**.

These small pictures are **icons**. Double-click an icon to open the program (or file) that it shows.

Icons that have a little arrow next to them (Outlook® and Word® shown here) are called **shortcuts**.

This is the 'Recycle Bin'. Files that you delete end up here (see p. 20).

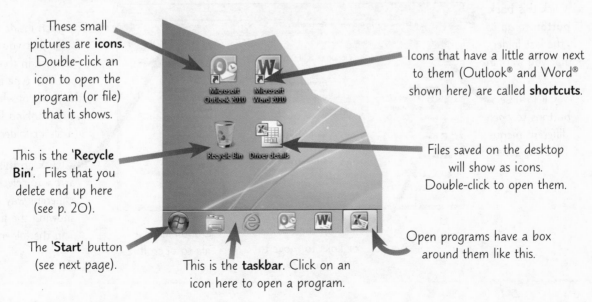

Files saved on the desktop will show as icons. Double-click to open them.

The 'Start' button (see next page).

This is the **taskbar**. Click on an icon here to open a program.

Open programs have a box around them like this.

Use the Start Menu to Find Software   EL3 L1 L2

1) Click on the '**Start**' button to open the **Start Menu**.

2) The Start Menu lets you get to the **different parts** of your computer.

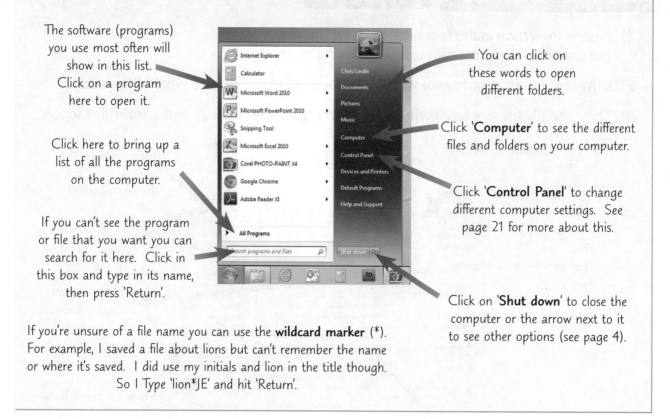

The software (programs) you use most often will show in this list. Click on a program here to open it.

Click here to bring up a list of all the programs on the computer.

If you can't see the program or file that you want you can search for it here. Click in this box and type in its name, then press 'Return'.

You can click on these words to open different folders.

Click '**Computer**' to see the different files and folders on your computer.

Click '**Control Panel**' to change different computer settings. See page 21 for more about this.

Click on '**Shut down**' to close the computer or the arrow next to it to see other options (see page 4).

If you're unsure of a file name you can use the **wildcard marker** (*). For example, I saved a file about lions but can't remember the name or where it's saved. I did use my initials and lion in the title though. So I Type 'lion*JE' and hit 'Return'.

Operating System Windows in Windows® 7   EL3 L1 L2

1) You can get to different folders by opening '**Computer**' (see above) and clicking to open the different folders.

2) The window below shows the files inside a folder in Windows® 7:

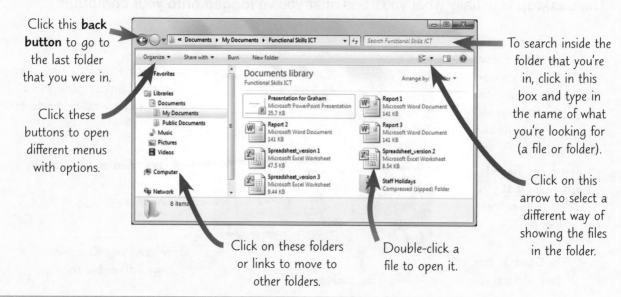

Click this **back button** to go to the last folder that you were in.

Click these buttons to open different menus with options.

To search inside the folder that you're in, click in this box and type in the name of what you're looking for (a file or folder).

Click on this arrow to select a different way of showing the files in the folder.

Click on these folders or links to move to other folders.

Double-click a file to open it.

Software (Program) Windows `EL3` `L1` `L2`

This is an example of a typical **Microsoft® Office® window**. Other software windows (from Microsoft® and other companies) will look different, but will have some similarities.

This top block of buttons and words is called a **ribbon**.

Click on these words, called **tabs** to change which toolbar (and buttons) is showing.

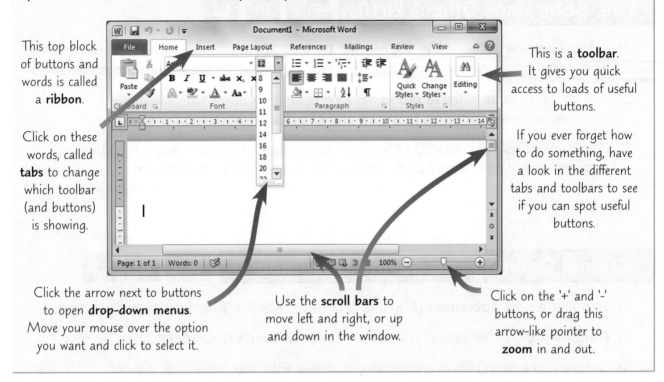

This is a **toolbar**. It gives you quick access to loads of useful buttons.

If you ever forget how to do something, have a look in the different tabs and toolbars to see if you can spot useful buttons.

Click the arrow next to buttons to open **drop-down menus**. Move your mouse over the option you want and click to select it.

Use the **scroll bars** to move left and right, or up and down in the window.

Click on the '+' and '-' buttons, or drag this arrow-like pointer to **zoom** in and out.

Practice Tasks

`EL3` `L1` `L2`

1) Using the Start Menu, find and open the program called '**Calculator**'.
   Use the buttons to work out 324 / 24. Write your answer below.

   ....

`EL3` `L1` `L2`

2) Which button would you click to close a window? Tick one box.

    ☐   ☐   ☐

`EL3` `L1` `L2`

3) Using the Start Menu, find '**Computer**' and click on it.

   a) Go to 'Libraries' and click on 'Pictures'.

   b) Open the folder called 'Sample Pictures'.

   c) Write down the names of any animal photos in the folder.

   You might not be able to answer this question — it'll depend on which operating system you have.

   ....

Office® Features and Shortcuts

This Book Uses Office® 2010   EL3 L1 L2

1) In this book we will be using **Microsoft® Office® 2010**.
   This set of programs includes Outlook®, Word®, Excel®, PowerPoint® and Access®.

2) The windows in all of these programs look alike (see page 13)
   and they all have **common features** and **shortcuts** explained here.

3) Other **versions** of Microsoft® Office® will be **similar**. Software made by other
   companies will have many of the same features but will look **different**.

Making, Opening and Saving Documents   EL3 L1 L2

1) To make a **new document** (**file**) in a program, click the 'File' tab, then click '**New**'.

2) **Double-click** on the option you want — usually '**Blank document**'.

3) To open an existing file in a program, click the '**File**' tab, then click '**Open**'.

4) A box will pop-up — use the **buttons**
   and **links** to find the file you want.

5) Click on the file, then on '**Open**'.
   Or **double-click** on the file.

6) Open files when you're not in a program by
   finding them in a folder and **double-clicking** them.

7) To **save** files, click the '**File**' tab, then click on '**Save**'.

8) Give the file a **name** and click '**Save**'. You need to use a **suitable name** (see p. 18).

9) You can also save files using '**Save As**'. Use this when you want to save a
   copy of the file with a different name. See page 18 for more about this.

You can Search for Text   EL3 L1 L2

1) You can use the '**Find**' tool to search for text or numbers.

2) Click on the '**Find**' button on the '**Home**' tab to open the 'Find' box.

3) **Type** what you want to search for, then press '**Enter**'.

4) **Where** the text appears in the file will be highlighted.
   If the text **can't be found** a message will tell you this.

Cut, Copy and Paste `EL3` `L1` `L2`

1) These **buttons** in the '**Home**' tab can be used to '**Cut**', '**Copy**' and '**Paste**'. They are found in all Office® programs.

2) **Select** what you want to **copy**, then click '**Copy**'. For example, select some text or a picture.

3) Select **where** you want the copied thing to go and click '**Paste**'.

4) '**Cut**' works in the same way as copy, but **removes** the original item at the same time.

5) You can use **drag** and **drop** to **move** things like files, text and pictures too.

6) Select what you want to move, then **click and drag** it with the **mouse** to a new place.

7) When you use drag and drop to move **files** it will often make a **copy** rather than **move** the original file.

Printing `EL3` `L1` `L2`

1) To print off documents, click the '**File**' tab, then click on '**Print**'.

2) A menu will open with **different settings** to choose from — these will be slightly different in each program but most of the ones shown below will be there:

Click this to print when you're happy with the settings.

Click this to choose your printer.

Click this to change the orientation of the page (portrait or landscape).

This lets you change the size of the page.

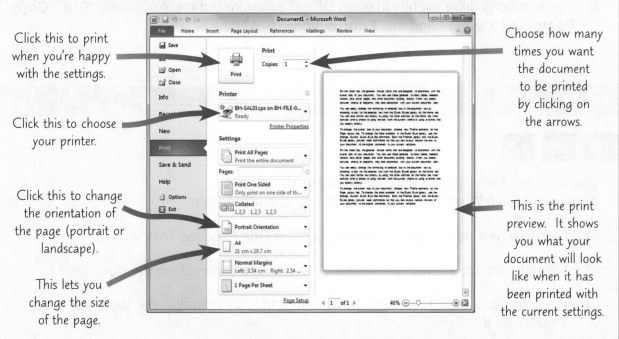

Choose how many times you want the document to be printed by clicking on the arrows.

This is the print preview. It shows you what your document will look like when it has been printed with the current settings.

Undo Changes with the Undo Button `EL3` `L1` `L2`

1) The '**Undo**' button is **above** the '**File**' tab.

2) In operating system windows (see page 12), click '**Organize**' to find the '**Undo**' button.

3) You can only undo a **certain number** of changes though, so don't rely on this.

Using Shortcuts EL3 L1 L2

1) You can use **shortcuts** to quickly do things on your computer.

2) There are **keyboard** shortcuts (shown in the table). To use them, **hold down** the first key(s), then press the final key(s), so they're all **held down together**.

Keyboard Shortcut	What it Does
Ctrl + C	Copy
Ctrl + V	Paste
Ctrl + X	Cut
Ctrl + S	Save
F12	Save As
Ctrl + F	Find
Ctrl + P	Print
Ctrl + Z	Undo

'Ctrl' is the 'Control' key (see p. 5).

3) **Right-clicking** in a program window is a really useful shortcut too — it brings up a **menu** with lots of **buttons**.

4) These buttons differ slightly in each Office® program but there's usually '**Cut**', '**Copy**', '**Paste**' and '**Delete**', and the '**Font**' buttons (p. 47).

Practice Tasks

EL3 L1 L2

1) Use the Start Menu to find and open 'Microsoft® Word®'.
If you don't have Word®, open your word processor program.

   a) Create a new document, then type 'Section One Practice Task' into it.

   b) Save the document with the name 'Section_One', then close the document.

   c) Open the document 'Section_One' again and type 'mistake' into the document. Then undo it.

   d) Save the file again and close the program.

EL3 L1 L2

2) Open the file called '**Office_Task**' and the file called '**Icon**'.

   a) Copy the picture from 'Icon' and paste it into the file called 'Office_Task'.

   b) Save the file 'Office_Task' to your desktop using a new sensible file name.

Using Storage Devices Safely

Files are Stored on the Hard Drive   EL3   L1   L2

To see what **files** (documents) are stored open '**Computer**' from the Start Menu:

Click on these to move to other folders.

This contains the files saved onto the computer's hard drive.

You can search for files and folders here. Just type the name you're looking for.

Removable storage devices will show up here.

Use Removable Storage Devices to Share Files   EL3   L1   L2

1) You can save files to **removable** storage devices and then **move them** between computers — just **connect** the devices to **other** computers to access them.

2) Examples of the devices include **CDs**, **DVD-Rs**, **Blu-rays**™, **memory cards** (from cameras and mobile phones) and **USB memory sticks** (also called pen drives).

3) These devices all connect to a computer **differently**. For example, **memory sticks** plug into **USB ports** on the computer unit that have this symbol next to them:

4) When connected, these devices show up in '**Computer**' under '**Devices with Removable Storage**'. **Double-click** to see the files on these devices.

5) You can **move files** to and from **memory sticks** and **cards** by using **drag and drop** or **copy and paste** (see page 15).

6) Memory sticks or cards should always be **ejected safely** to make sure that **no data** is **lost or damaged**.

7) To eject safely, click the '**Safely Remove Hardware and Eject Media**' icon on the task bar, then click '**Eject**' for the device you want to remove.

Click this 'Safely Remove...' icon to open the 'eject' menu.

If the icon doesn't appear, click this arrow.

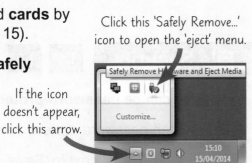

Practice Task

EL3   L1   L2

1) Describe how to safely remove a memory stick from your computer.

....

....

Managing Files and Folders

Saving and Naming Files `EL3` `L1` `L2`

1) You can use 'Save' and 'Save As' to save files in most programs (see p. 14).

2) Use 'Save As' to save a **copy** of the file or **change where** it's saved.

3) You should give files sensible, **correctly-spelt** names, which describe what the document is.

> We use underscores (_) in place of spaces in our file naming in this book but you don't necessarily have to.

4) In the test, names should describe the **task scenario**. For example, use 'Task 1 Bird Poster' not 'Test'.

5) Ask your **tutor** if you need to use anything like your name, initials or the date too.

6) When you **save as** you can also choose which **file type** to save it as. For example, you might want to save something as a web page.

7) Click on the box next to the words '**Save as type**' to get a list of different file types you can save it as.

File name: Hotel booking details
Save as type: Word Document
Authors:
~~Word Document~~
Word Macro-Enabled Document
Word 97-2003 Document
Word Template
Word Macro-Enabled Template
Word 97-2003 Template

Click on the file type you want.

8) Different file types are shown by different **file extensions**. These are the **letters** that come **after** the file **name**.

9) Here are some **common** file extensions:

File Extension	What Type of File
.txt	Text document
.htm .html	Web page
.jpg .png .gif	Images
.mp3 .wav	Sound

File Extension	What Type of File
.docx	Word® document
.xlsx	Excel® spreadsheet
.accdb	Access® database
.pptx	PowerPoint® document

File Security `L1` `L2`

1) Files can be **password-protected**. To open them you'll need a password (see p. 7).

2) You can password-protect a file from the '**Save As**' window.

3) Click on '**Tools**' next to 'Save', then click 'General Options...'.

Tools ▼ | Save
Map Network Drive...
Save Options...
General Options...
Web Options...

4) **Type** in the password into the '**to open**' box and press '**OK**'. **Retype** your password and press 'OK' again. The file is now password-protected.

5) Files can be also made '**Read-only**', which means people **can't** save **changes** to it.

6) To make a file '**Read-only**', **right-click** on the file itself, then click '**Properties**'.

7) Click the 'Read-only' checkbox in the **Attributes** section of the '**General**' tab and then click '**OK**'.

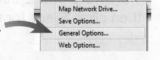

Attributes: ☑ Read-only   ☐ Hidden

Files are Organised into Folders   EL3 L1 L2

1) **Folders** help you organise your files (documents).

2) To make **new folders**, click the '**New folder**' button in the window where you want the files to be stored.

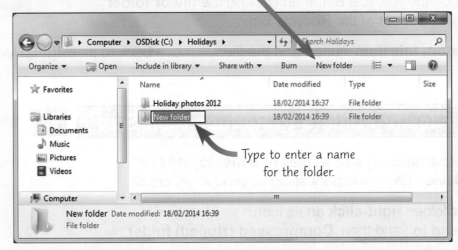

Double-click on a folder to see what's inside it.

Type to enter a name for the folder.

See page 12 for more about searching for files and folders.

3) Or **right-click** somewhere that isn't an icon in the place where you want the folder to go, then click '**New**', then '**Folder**'. For example, on your desktop.

4) Make sure folders are **sensibly named too** (see previous page).

5) **Rename** folders by **right-clicking** on them, click '**Rename**', then **type** the new name.

6) **Move** files and folders using '**Cut**' or '**Copy**' and '**Paste**', or **drag** and **drop** (see p 15).

7) To **delete** a file or folder, **click** on it, then press the '**Delete**' key.

8) Then click '**Yes**' in the box that appears.

9) In the test you might be asked to make a **folder structure** to store your work in:

Example

Chris is taking the Functional Skills ICT test. As part of this, he has made some documents about a bakery business. He has been asked to store all his work in a new folder using sensible folder and file names. He has taken a screen shot to show his folder and files:

Here are his three sensibly-named files.

1) He saved his work in 'ICT Documents' in a folder called '**ICT Test Tasks**'.

2) To get a **screen shot** showing what's inside the folder, he just **double-clicked** on the folder then pressed '**PrtScn**' — see p. 24.

Deleting Files and Folders   EL3   L1   L2

1) When files or folders are **deleted** they are sent to the **Recycle Bin** on the desktop.

2) If you **accidentally** delete something you can **get it back**.

3) **Double-click** on the Recycle Bin, then click on the **file or folder** you want to get back out of the Recycle Bin.

4) Click the '**Restore this item**' button and the file will move back to its **original** location.

You can Zip Files or Folders to Reduce their Size   L2

1) Zipped files are **smaller** in size so they're **better** to add to a **removable device** (like a memory stick) or send in an **email**.

2) To zip a file or folder, **right-click** on its icon.
   Then click '**Send to**', and then '**Compressed (zipped) folder**':

| Send to | ▶ | 📋 Compressed (zipped) folder |
| Cut | | 💻 Desktop (create shortcut) |

3) A **new** zipped folder will appear in the **same place** as the **original** one.
   Name it **sensibly** (see p. 18).

4) **Double-click** on a **zipped folder** to open it and see the files inside.

5) But you need to **unzip and extract** the files from it before you can **change** them.

6) To **unzip** a folder, **right-click** on it, then click '**Extract All**'.

7) Choose **where** you want the unzipped files to **go** by clicking '**Browse**'.
   Click OK, then '**Extract**' when you've finished.

Practice Tasks

EL3   L1   L2

1) Open the file '**File_1**'.

   a) Create a folder on your desktop named 'Reading'.

   b) Use 'Save As' to name 'File_1' more sensibly and save it in your 'Reading' folder.

L1   L2

2) For this question you'll need the files called '**Bread_photos**' and '**Bread_list**'.

   a) In 'Documents' create a new, sensibly-named folder and put the files in it.

   b) Password-protect the file 'Bread_photos' and take a screen shot to show this. See p. 24 for screen shots.

   c) Make the file 'Bread_list' read-only and take a screen shot to show this.

Changing Settings

You can Change Lots of Settings on Your Computer L1 L2

1) You can use the '**Control Panel**' to **change** different **computer settings**.
   For example you can change the size of text and icons.

2) In Windows® 7, open the **Start Menu**, then click '**Control Panel**' (see page 12).

3) Click on a **green** category to see more options,
   or click on one of the **blue** options to go straight to the chosen setting:

Click here to check the network settings and internet connection.

Click here to change settings for hardware attached to your computer. This includes volume settings for speakers, and settings for your mouse and printer.

Click here to change how this screen looks.

Click here to change how your desktop looks. This includes the screen resolution (how clear and sharp information on your screen looks).

Click here to make changes for people with impairments (like eye-sight issues).

Control Panel ▸

Search Control Panel

Adjust your computer's settings

View by: Category ▾

System and Security
Review your computer's status
Back up your computer
Find and fix problems

Network and Internet
View network status and tasks
Choose homegroup and sharing options

Hardware and Sound
View devices and printers
Add a device

Programs
Uninstall a program
Get programs

User Accounts
Change account type

Appearance and Personalization
Change the theme
Change desktop background
Adjust screen resolution

Clock, Language, and Region
Change keyboards or other input methods
Change display language

Ease of Access
Let Windows suggest settings
Optimize visual display

4) To help people with eye-sight problems, use the blue '**Optimise visual display**' link
   to **increase** the **size** of text and icons, and to turn on the **magnifier** tool.

5) To help people with **hearing problems** you can change things in '**Ease of Access**'
   too — like make any spoken information show on the screen as text.

6) You can also do things like make the **speed** you need to double-click slower.

7) You can also change some settings using the right-hand side of the **task bar**.
   For example, click on the **speaker** icon (◁») and **drag** the slider to change **volume**.

Practice Task

1) a)   State one way that you can adjust the settings on your computer to make it easier
         for a visually-impaired person to use.

         ....

   b)   State one setting that could be changed to make the mouse easier to use.

         ....

Minimising Physical Stress

You Should Sit Properly at a Computer   EL3 L1 L2

Using a computer for a **long time** can be **uncomfortable**. So make sure you **set up** your work area **properly**:

The top of the monitor should be at eye level or just below and about an arm's length away from you.

Your keyboard should be just below elbow level so there is minimal bend at your wrists.

Adjust your chair so you're sitting with a straight back.

You should keep your elbows close to your body and at an angle around 90-120°.

Your backrest should be adjusted so it supports your lower back.

The front of your seat shouldn't be pressing into the back of your knees.

Your feet should be flat on the floor or resting on a footrest if they don't reach the floor.

Your chair should be an adjustable swivel chair — it should spin round, be height adjustable and have an adjustable backrest.

1) Make sure you can **reach everything you need** without having to **stretch** or **strain**.

2) Take **regular breaks** and frequently **look away** from your monitor, **walk** around and **exercise** your fingers to **reduce** the **health risks** of working with computers.

3) Make sure there's plenty of **light** where you are working but **no glare** on your monitor.

4) Change your monitor's **contrast** and **brightness settings** to help stop **eye strain**.

Practice Task

EL3 L1 L2

1) a) Set up your computer work area properly.

   b) Suggest one change you can make to your monitor to help prevent eye strain.

Printing and Capturing Evidence

You'll Need to Give Evidence of Your Work EL3 L1 L2

1) In the **test** you'll be asked to give **evidence** to show that you did the tasks.

2) You can be asked for **different types** of evidence, such as:

   - A saved or printed file (document).
   - A saved or printed screen shot.
   - Information or a screen shot added into an evidence document.

3) Make sure that the **evidence** you give fully **answers** the test **question**.

4) Save your evidence with a **sensible name** and in a **suitable place**.
   The name you choose should describe what the file is (see p. 18 for more).

5) Make sure any **text**, **handwriting** or **images** are clear and big enough to **read easily**.

Printing EL3 L1 L2

1) In the test you could be asked to **print off** evidence.

2) Make sure that **all** the **information** you need is on the **printout**.
   For example, you might be asked to add your name as a footer on every page.

3) Make sure you follow any **printing instructions**.
   For example, A4 landscape or 2 pages per sheet.

4) **Check** your **printouts** to make sure they are **correct** and you can **read** everything.
   For example, if you're printing a spreadsheet make sure the columns
   are wide enough so that you can see the data inside them (see page 65).

Printing Problems EL3 L1 L2

If a file **isn't printing**, make sure that:

- The printer is **turned on**.

- All the **printer cables** are connected properly
  or the printer is connected to your **wireless network**.

- The printer hasn't run out of **ink**, **toner** or **paper**.

- Paper hasn't **jammed** in the printer.

- The file has been sent to the **correct printer**.

Screen Shots EL3 L1 L2

1) You might be asked to produce **screen shots** of your work.
   (They can also be called **screen prints**, **screen dumps** or **screen captures**.)

2) A screen shot is where you take an **image** of what is **showing** on your **screen**.

3) So make sure you have the **right** file or window open when you take one.

4) To take a **screen shot**, press the **print screen** key '**PrtScn**', then use
   '**Paste**' to add it into a document. For example, a word processing file.

See page 5 to see where the print screen key is on the keyboard.

5) **Microsoft® Word®** also has a **screen shot tool**.

6) Click the '**Insert**' tab, then click '**Screenshot**'.
   Then click to choose which **window** you want to screen shot.

Screenshot

7) You might need to '**Crop**' and **increase** the **size** of a screen shot
   to make it large enough for the right information to be **read**.

8) Look at pages 55-56 to see how to do this for any **graphic**.

9) You should only have **two** screen shots **per page**, and **increase** their **size** so they
   take up as much space as they can — this should mean they can be **read easily**.

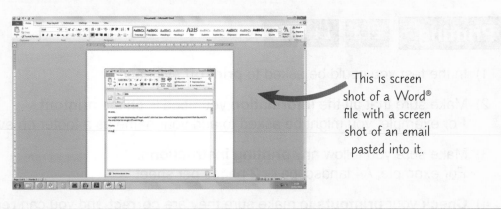

This is screen shot of a Word® file with a screen shot of an email pasted into it.

Practice Task

EL3 L1 L2

1) Open the file called '**Evidence**'.

   a) Insert a screen shot of the first page of the file into the
      correct place on the second page.

   b) Answer the question on the second page.
      Type your answer into the correct place on the second page.

   c) Print the document in landscape orientation.

   d) Save the document with a sensible name.

   e) Close the program.

Searching the Internet

The Internet   EL3 L1 L2

1) The **internet** is a worldwide network of **computers** all **linked together**.

2) Any computer can **connect** to the internet (some gadgets like mobile phones can too).

3) If you're on the internet, you can do lots of things — look at **websites** and **web pages**, send **emails**, **download** images, movies and music...

A website is lots of web pages linked together.

Internet Browsers   EL3 L1 L2

1) To **look** at web pages, you need to use a **browser**.

2) Browser icons are usually found on the **desktop** or in the **task bar**.

3) A common browser is **Microsoft® Internet Explorer®**.

4) When you **click** on a browser it will open a **window** a bit like this:

Use the back or forward buttons to flick between pages.

Click on the tabs to open more pages.

You can set a certain web page to open when you click on the browser — this is called your home page. This button takes you back to it.

Address bar.

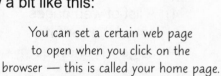

To stop a page opening, click the stop button (X). To refresh a page, click ↻ .

When you're on a page, click here to 'bookmark' it or save it as a 'favourite'. You might need to click 'Add to favourites' too.

The web page will show here.

Click here, then 'File' and 'Save as...' to save the page. Use the extension .htm or .html.

Getting to Web Pages   EL3 L1 L2

1) Web pages have **addresses**, called **URLs**. For example, the URL or web address for the CGP books website is https://www.cgpbooks.co.uk.

URLs usually start with 'http://' or 'https://' but you can just start with 'www'.

2) **Type** a URL into the **address bar,** press '**Return**' and the page opens.

3) Another way to get to a web page is to **click** on a **link** (or **hyperlink**).

4) A link is an **image** or **piece of text** which takes you to a web page when you click on it. Link text is often **coloured** and **underlined**, like <u>this</u>.

5) To save URLs, you can '**Copy**' and '**Paste**' them into documents. Or make the web page a '**favourite**'.

Search Engines EL3 L1 L2

1) You can use a **search engine** to **find** a web page or some information. For example, to find the CGP Books website or some train times.

2) Popular search engines are **Google**™, **Yahoo!** and **Bing**.

3) **Type words** into the **search bar** of a search engine. It will then **list** web pages where those words **appear**.

4) The pages that **match** the words **best** come up **first**.

Example

To find the CGP Books website:

1) Open a **browser window**, type 'www.google.co.uk' into the **address bar** and press '**Return**'.

2) Type 'cgp books' into the **search bar**.

3) Press '**Return**' or click on the **search button**.

4) A list of web pages called the **results page** will show up.

5) Click on a **link** to visit the website that suits you best.

Sometimes the first couple of 'results' on the results page will be adverts.

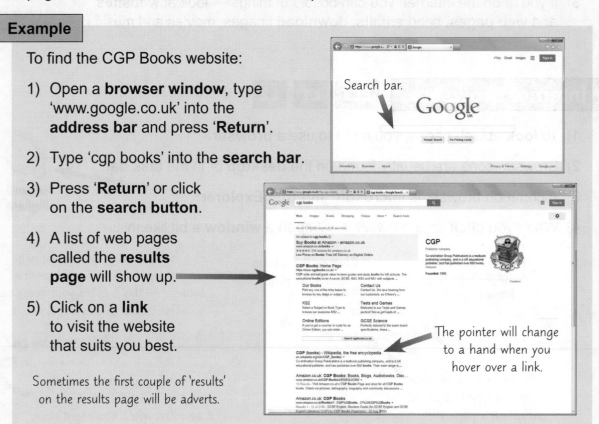

Search bar.

The pointer will change to a hand when you hover over a link.

How to Search Effectively Using Keywords EL3 L1 L2

1) The **words** you type into the **search bar** are called **keywords**.

If you're asked for evidence of your search criteria, use the results page with the keywords showing.

2) The **better** your choice of **keywords**, the **better** the **search** will be.

3) Search engines often **ignore** words like 'the', 'a', 'he', 'she', and they **don't** understand **questions**.

4) You need to think about what **words** might **appear** on the page you're **looking for**.

5) A good way to **practise** searching is:

   • Think of a **question** you'd like to **ask**.

   • Use **only** the **most important** words of the question as **keywords**.

   • See what **results** come up. If they aren't good, try **adding**, **changing** or **deleting** keywords.

Example 1

To find out what Michael Jackson's **date of birth** is:

1) Pick the **most important** words as the keywords — Michael Jackson.

2) Type these into a **search engine**.

3) This gives some good results but the search could be **better**.
   Try **adding** a third **keyword** — birth.

Example 2

1) How do you **convert** from miles to kilometres?

2) Use the **keywords** 'convert miles kilometres'.

3) Click on the **most useful** link.

6) The **URL** for a **web page** is **different** to the URL for the **search** for the web page.

7) Make sure you give the **right one** in the **test**. For example, 'https://www.cgpbooks.co.uk/' is the CGP URL, 'https://www.google.co.uk/#q=cgp+books' is the search URL.

Practice Tasks

`EL3` `L1` `L2`

1) Liz has a new car and wants to find a comparison website for car insurance quotes. What keywords should Liz use to search for one?

....

`EL3` `L1` `L2`

2) Use the internet to find out the following:

a) The postal address of The National Archives.

....

b) The phone number of West Midlands Safari Park.

....

`L2`

3) Alan uses the website www.wesellthings.com a lot. He wants to bookmark it. Describe how Alan can do this.

....

Navigating Within Websites   EL3 L1 L2

1) You might need to **find** information **within** a **website**.

2) Websites can have lots of web pages, so you'll need to go to the **right page** first.

3) Websites are **all different** but here are some things to **look out for**:

Use the back and forward buttons to flick between pages.

Lots of websites have their own search bar. Enter keywords to get results within that website.

Click on text, picture or box links to go to different pages.

Most websites will have lots of menus that drop-down if you click on them. Click on parts of the menu to move to different pages.

4) To find specific information on a web page, also look out for keywords:

- Press '**Ctrl**' and '**F**' to bring up a search box to find words on that page.

- Make sure you look at the whole page — **scroll up** and **down** if needed.

5) People **don't** usually **read** a web page **evenly** from top to bottom. They often look **more** at certain areas. For example, areas near logos at the **top** or areas that **stand out more** than others.

6) These areas are sometimes called **hotspots**.

7) Companies often **design** their websites with these hotspots in mind.

Images you can click on which link to other places can also be called hotspots.

Searching for Images and Maps   EL3 L1 L2

1) You can use some search engines to find **images** and **maps**.

2) In Google™, click on the '**Images**' or '**Maps**' button, just **below** the **search bar** on the **results page**.

Or you could use 'map' as one of the keywords.

Google   united kingdom

Web Maps Images News Videos More ▾ Search tools

3) Click on the image you like and **click again** to go to the **web page** the image is on.

4) To **save** the image, **right click** and select '**Save picture as...**'.

5) To **copy** the image, **right click** and select '**Copy**'. Then '**Paste**' it wherever you like.

Advanced Searches

1) Search engines have **advanced search options** for doing more **specific** searches.

2) You usually **click** an icon on the search engine to **open** the advanced search page.

3) In Google™, click this icon in the **top right** of the search results screen:

4) You can also use these **marks** (operators) with
your keywords to carry out a **better search**:

" "	To search for an exact word or phrase.
OR	To search for one word OR another.
–	To search for things but excluding the word after this.
*	To search for an unknown term.

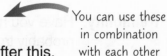 You can use these in combination with each other too.

Examples

1) To search for opening times at Alton Towers, try using quote marks:
type **Alton Towers "opening times"** into the search bar.

2) For information on Olympic games held in London or Berlin try using OR:
Olympic games London OR Berlin.

3) For a restaurant in Leeds that's not an Italian: **Restaurant Leeds -Italian**.

4) To find the middle name of someone famous: **Jamie * Curtis**.

Practice Tasks

EL3 L1 L2

1) You've been asked to produce a leaflet about the Lake District National Park.
Find the following to include in the leaflet:

a) A picture of the mountain called Old Man of Coniston.
Save it to your desktop using a suitable file name.

b) A map of Lake Windermere. Print out a screen shot of your search for the map.

c) The opening times of The Pencil Museum in Keswick. Write the answer below.

....

L1 L2

2) Billy wants a new car, either a Vauxhall Corsa or Astra. He'd like to read some information about them both first. Carry out an internet search to find suitable websites for Billy. Paste a screen shot of your results into a word processing file and save it with a suitable file name.

Choosing the Right Information

Choosing a Website you can Trust `EL3` `L1` `L2`

1) Anyone can put **anything** on the internet.

2) So you need to use **websites** you can **trust**.

3) Here are some things to **look for**:

Reliability: Have you heard of the website? Is it an official one? For example, you can probably trust a news story on the BBC website more than one on a blog.

Currency: When was the website created or last updated? This will tell you how up-to-date the information is.

A blog is a website where people can write their opinions for others to read.

Relevance: Make sure the website is relevant to you. For example, if you want information on Birmingham, England, make sure you're not on a website for Birmingham, Alabama, USA.

Bias: Who wrote the page? People can write things in a biased way to make a point. For example, a company website might only post positive reviews of its products.

Copyright `EL3` `L1` `L2`

1) Text, audio, video, music, song lyrics and images are protected by **copyright laws**.

2) This means it's **illegal** to use them without **asking** the copyright holder's **permission**.

3) You also might have to **pay** to use it and you **always** have to **acknowledge** the holder.

4) Look out for these **copyright notices**:

- The © **symbol**. For example, BBC © 2014 on a page means the BBC owns the copyright.

- **Watermarks** or **names** on images. These tell you someone owns it.

- **Copyright-free** or **public domain** notes. Work that says it's copyright-free or in the public domain can used **without permission**. You should still **acknowledge** the owner though. Look out for **license terms**. For example, Creative Commons licenses.

It's OK to use basic facts like dates, addresses and opening times without permission.

Internet Behaviour `EL3` `L1` `L2`

A troll is someone who uses the internet to upset or harass others.

1) You should **behave** on the internet as you would in **real life**.

2) This means being **polite** and **respectful** of other people and their views.

3) **Don't** make **threatening**, **abusive** or **racist** comments — don't become a **troll**.

4) **Don't argue** with people or use **capitals** — that means you're **shouting**.

Internet Safety `EL3` `L1` `L2`

1) **Criminals** can get information from **emails** and the **internet**.

2) So **do not** give out **personal information** unless it's to a **trusted** source.
   For example, your bank's secure website should be okay, but a forum probably isn't.

3) You should be **very careful** when giving out dates of birth, addresses,
   email addresses, telephone numbers or bank details.

4) The **Data Protection Act** sets **rules** for how **companies** deal with
   personal information.

5) **Viruses** can enter your computer from the internet.

6) So installing and running **antivirus software** on your computer is important.

7) Be careful **downloading** or opening **files**, especially if you don't know where they're from.

8) **Don't** click on links in **pop-ups** (web pages which 'pop-up' without you going to them).

Electronic Communication `EL3` `L1` `L2`

Because of the internet we can now **communicate** easily with people all over the world.

1) **Email** — can be used to send information quickly and easily.

2) Websites that allow **file sharing** — multiple people can work on something
   at the same time, or pick up files from
   a shared place. For example, Dropbox™.

3) **Instant messaging** — allows people to talk instantly. For example, a company can
   answer a customer's question on a website straight away.

4) **Blogs** and **online forums** — people can easily share their views and read others' too.

5) **Social media** — allows people to stay in touch with lots of
   other people. For example, Facebook® and Twitter.

Practice Tasks

`EL3` `L1` `L2`

1) In which of these cases is it safe to give out your personal information? Tick one box.

☐ A clothes website for a shop you've never heard of based in another country.

☐ Your secure banking website.

☐ On a blog.

☐ On a forum.

`EL3` `L1` `L2`

2) Sunita is setting up a new business and is looking for advice on the internet.
She finds two websites: a UK government one and a blog of someone who works in a bank.
Which website will be more reliable? Give a reason for your answer.

....

....

....

`L1` `L2`

3) Maria is making flyers advertising walking holidays in Yorkshire. She finds these images on
the internet. Which image can she use without permission? Give a reason for your answer.

A

Tommy's Tours

B

Fred Tetley © 2014.

C

This work is in
the public domain.

....

....

....

Sending and Receiving Emails

Emails are Electronic Messages   EL3   L1   L2

1) You can use **email** to send a **message** to one person or a group of people.

2) Sending an email is a bit like sending a letter but instead of printing it out and sending it on paper, you send it **electronically** using a **computer**.

You can send emails from phones, tablets and other gadgets too.

3) To send or receive an email you need to have an **email address**.

Examples

chris@cgpbooks.co.uk ⬅ *Email addresses always have an @ symbol in them. They never have spaces in them.*

matt287@cgpbooks.com ⬅

Reading Email   EL3   L1   L2

1) To **read** your email you need to use **software** (such as Microsoft® Outlook®).

2) In this section the **screenshots** show what using email in **Outlook**® looks like. **Other software** and **websites** might **look different** but will **work in a similar way**.

3) When emails are sent to your email address they go into your **inbox**. You can **open** and **read** them there.

Example

This is what an inbox looks like in Outlook®.

The inbox is highlighted here. This shows that you are seeing what's in your inbox.

To open an email, click on it and it will appear on the right of the screen.

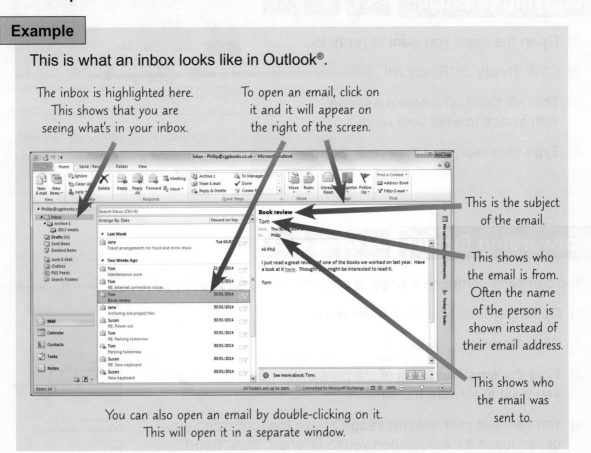

This is the subject of the email.

This shows who the email is from. Often the name of the person is shown instead of their email address.

This shows who the email was sent to.

You can also open an email by double-clicking on it. This will open it in a separate window.

Sending Email EL3 L1 L2

1) Click on the '**New E-mail**' button on the '**Home**' tab. A window will open with a **blank** message.

2) **Type** the **email address** of the person you're sending the email to. To do this you type an email address next to where it says '**To...**'. You can send an email to **several people** by typing in all their email addresses here.

3) Add a **subject** to the email — this is a few words to **describe** what the email is about.

4) Type your **message** (or **paste** text into here from somewhere else).

5) Send your email by clicking on '**Send**'.

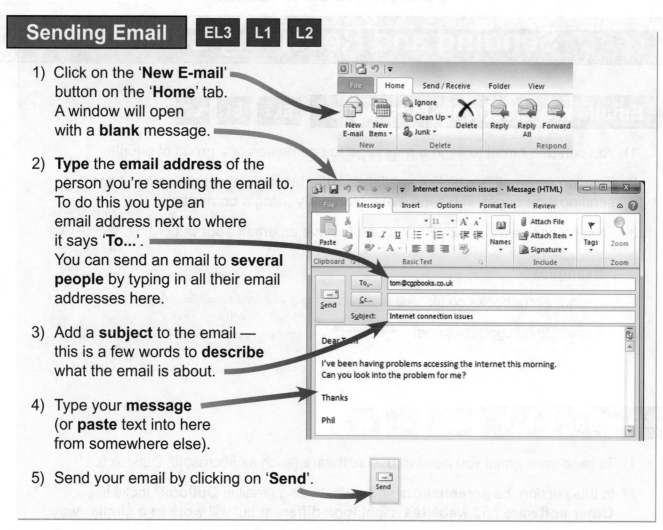

Replying to Email EL3 L1 L2

1) **Open** the email you want to **reply** to.

2) Click '**Reply**' or '**Reply All**'.

3) This will bring up a **new message** with **space** to write your reply.

4) **Type** your reply and then click '**Send**'.

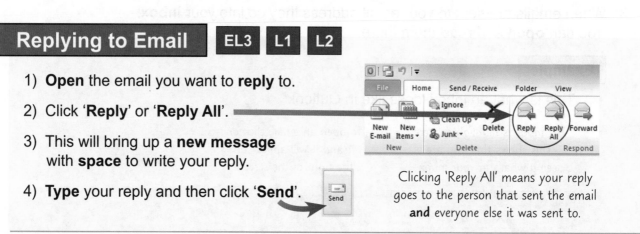

Clicking 'Reply All' means your reply goes to the person that sent the email **and** everyone else it was sent to.

Forwarding Email EL3 L1 L2

You can send someone a **copy** of an email using **forwarding**.

1) **Open** the email you want to **forward**.

2) Click '**Forward**'.

3) Type the **email address** of the person (or people) you want to forward the email to.

4) You can add your own **message** above the forwarded email or just leave it blank. When you're finished, click '**Send**'.

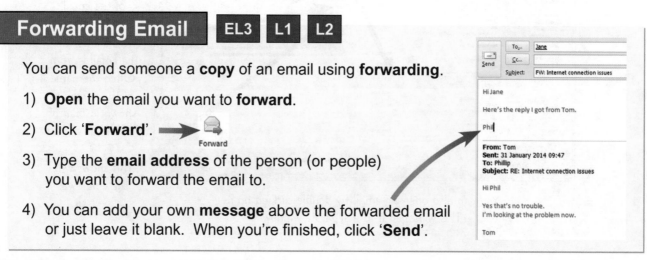

Attaching Files to Emails `L1` `L2`

You can **attach files** to emails.
They're then sent with the message.

To attach a file to an email:

1) Click the button marked '**Attach File**'
   on the '**Message**' tab of the email window.

2) Find the file that you want to attach
   and click '**Insert**'.

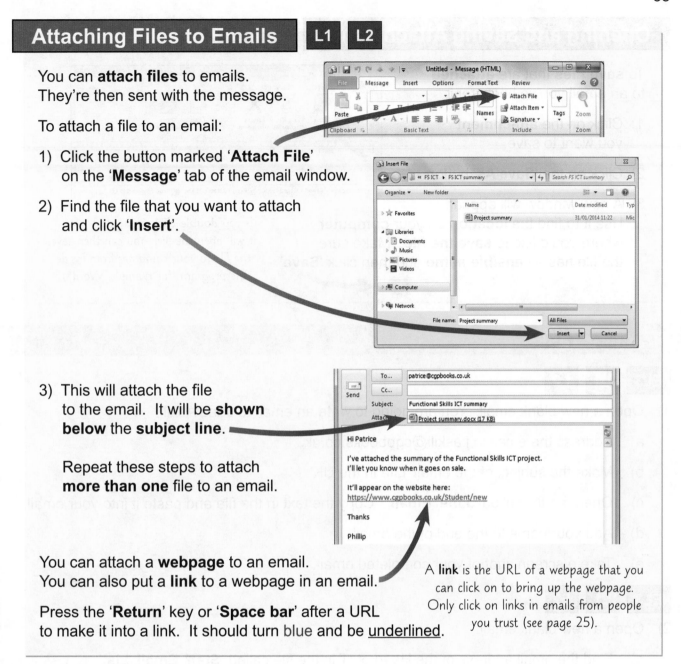

3) This will attach the file
   to the email. It will be **shown
   below** the **subject line**.

   Repeat these steps to attach
   more than one file to an email.

You can attach a **webpage** to an email.
You can also put a **link** to a webpage in an email.

Press the '**Return**' key or '**Space bar**' after a URL
to make it into a link. It should turn blue and be <u>underlined</u>.

> A **link** is the URL of a webpage that you
> can click on to bring up the webpage.
> Only click on links in emails from people
> you trust (see page 25).

Attaching Compressed Folders `L2`

1) Attaching files to an email makes it **bigger**. This means it takes **longer** to send.

2) To help **reduce** this problem you can attach files in **compressed (zip) folders**
   — see page 20 for more about these folders.

3) **Compressed folders** also make it **easier** to attach **more than one** file to an email
   — you only need to attach one compressed folder instead of lots of separate files.

4) Attach compressed folders to an email in the **same way** as you'd attach normal files.
   When they are attached they will be shown in the same way too.

Opening and Saving Attachments L1 L2

To **save files** that are **attached** to an email you've been sent:

1) Click on the **attachment** you want to save.

2) Click on the '**Save As**' button.

3) A new window will appear. Use it to find the **location** on your **computer** where you'd like to **save the file**. Make sure the file has a **sensible name** and then click '**Save**'.

If you **double-click** on an attachment it will open the file. You can then save the file to your computer from inside the program (for example, Word®).

Practice Tasks

EL3 L1 L2

1) Open a new blank email. You are going to write an email to Jane Askill.

   a) Address the email to j.askill@cgpbooks.co.uk.

   b) Make the subject of the email 'Life in the UK'.

   c) Open the file called '**Jane_Email**'. Copy the text in the file and paste it into your email.

   d) Add your name to the end of the email.

   e) Take a screen shot of your completed email.

EL3 L1 L2

2) Open a new blank email.

   a) Find the email address of the Head of IT in the file called '**Staff_Email_List**'. Address your email to this person.

   b) Make the subject of the email 'New PCs'.

   c) Open the file called '**IT_Email**'. Copy the text in the file and paste it into your email.

   d) Add your name to the end of the email.

   e) Take a screen shot of your completed email.

L1 L2

3) Open a new blank email. You are going to write an email to Susan.

   a) Address the email to susan@cgpbooks.co.uk.

   b) Make the subject of the email 'Hallway painting'.

   c) Open the file called '**Susan_Email**'. Copy the text in the file and paste it into your email.

   d) Attach the file '**wet_paint_sign**' to the email.

   e) Take a screen shot of your completed email.

Contacts Lists

Using your Contacts List L1 L2

1) Your **contacts list** is where you **store** the **details** of people that you send email to.

2) It's basically a **list** of people's **names** and their **email addresses**, but you can also store other details about people such as their phone numbers and address.

3) You can get to your contacts list by clicking on the '**Contacts**' button. (It's at the **bottom left** of the Outlook® window.)

4) In **Outlook**® your contacts list will look like this.

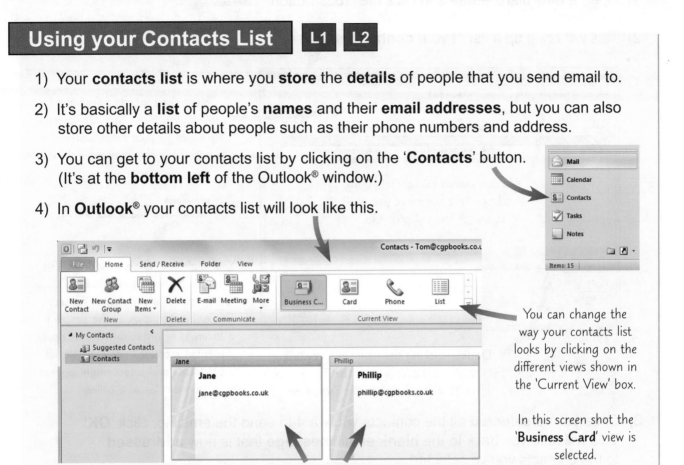

You can change the way your contacts list looks by clicking on the different views shown in the 'Current View' box.

In this screen shot the '**Business Card**' view is selected.

Here are two different contacts.

Adding New Contact Details L2

1) Click '**New Contact**' which is on the '**Home**' tab.

   A new contact **window** will appear.

2) **Fill** in the **details** that you want to add, such as name and email address. In this example, details have been filled in for a new contact called Miriam.

   Click on the '**Full Name...**' button to get more name options to fill in.

3) When you've added all the details you want to, click the '**Save & Close**' button to save the contact details into your contacts list.

   There are lots of other details that you can fill in for a contact. For example, different phone numbers.

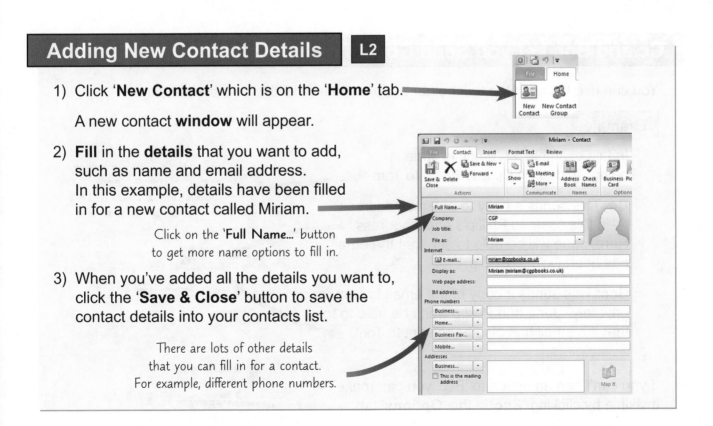

Sending an Email to One or More Contacts `L1` `L2`

1) Open a **new** blank **email** and click the '**To...**' button.

2) This will bring up a list of your **contacts**.

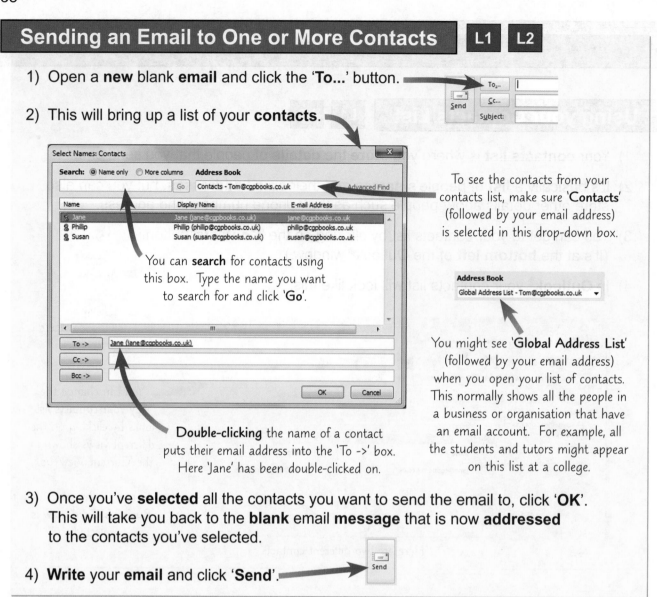

To see the contacts from your contacts list, make sure '**Contacts**' (followed by your email address) is selected in this drop-down box.

Address Book
Global Address List - Tom@cgpbooks.co.uk ▼

You might see '**Global Address List**' (followed by your email address) when you open your list of contacts. This normally shows all the people in a business or organisation that have an email account. For example, all the students and tutors might appear on this list at a college.

You can **search** for contacts using this box. Type the name you want to search for and click '**Go**'.

Double-clicking the name of a contact puts their email address into the 'To ->' box. Here 'Jane' has been double-clicked on.

3) Once you've **selected** all the contacts you want to send the email to, click '**OK**'. This will take you back to the **blank** email **message** that is now **addressed** to the contacts you've selected.

4) **Write** your **email** and click '**Send**'.

Cc and Bcc Let you Send Copies of Emails to People `L1` `L2`

You can use **Cc** and **Bcc** to let other people see emails that you are sending.

Example

In this example, an email to Jane is being Cc'd to Phillip and Bcc'd to Tom.

Cc: This sends a copy to an email address — in this case, to Phillip's email address. Here, Jane will be able to see that the email has been Cc'd to Phillip.

Bcc: This sends a copy of the email to someone privately. Jane and Phillip won't be able to tell that the email has also been sent to Tom.

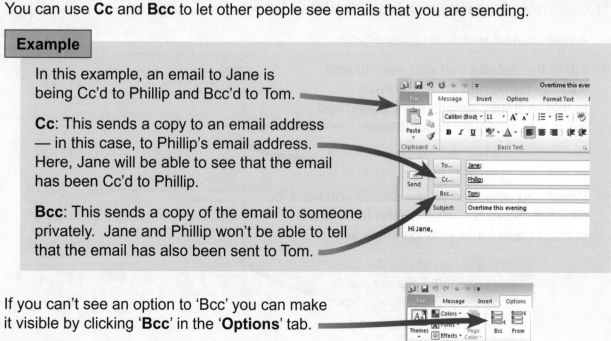

If you can't see an option to 'Bcc' you can make it visible by clicking '**Bcc**' in the '**Options**' tab.

Creating Group Distribution Lists L2

A **group distribution list** (called a 'Contact Group' in Outlook®) is a list of **email addresses** saved under **one name**. They can be useful when you want to send an email to a particular group of people — for example, people who work in your building or are on your course.

1) Open your **contacts list**.

2) Click on '**New Contact Group**' on the '**Home**' tab.

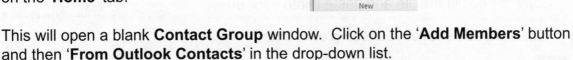

This will open a blank **Contact Group** window. Click on the '**Add Members**' button and then '**From Outlook Contacts**' in the drop-down list.

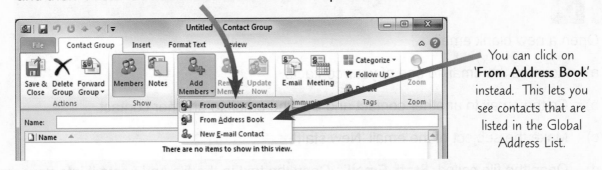

You can click on '**From Address Book**' instead. This lets you see contacts that are listed in the Global Address List.

3) **Add** contacts to the group by **double-clicking** on them.

Contacts that you've added to the group will appear here.

4) After clicking '**OK**', you'll see a window that shows the members in the group. Type a **name** for the group and then click '**Save & Close**'.

Type a name for the group here.

Members of the group are listed here.

5) The group will then **appear** in your **contacts list**. To send an email to the group, follow the method shown on the previous page.

Practice Tasks

L1 **L2**

1) Open a new blank email.

   a) Address the email to three people in your contacts list or address book.

   b) Make the subject of the email 'Plumber needed'.

   c) Open the file called '**Plumber_Email**'.
   Copy the text in the file and paste it into your email.

   d) Take a screen shot of your completed email.

> *You need to have some contacts saved to answer this question, or search for some on the Global Address List.*

L1 **L2**

2) Open a new blank email.

   a) Address the email to one of your contacts.

   b) Cc the email to another contact and Bcc the email to another contact.

   c) Make the subject of the email 'New staff'.

   d) Open the file called '**Staff_Email**'. Copy the text in the file and paste it into your email.

   e) Take a screen shot of your completed email.

L2

3) Open the file called '**Contact_Details**'.

   a) Open a new contact window. Create a new contact for Daniel including all the details you've been given. Take a screen shot of the window and then save the contact.

   b) Open a new contact window. Create a new contact for Nadine including all the details you've been given. Take a screen shot of the window and then save the contact.

   c) Create a new group distribution list and add the two contacts you've made (Daniel and Nadine). Name the list 'Team A'.

   d) Take a screen shot of the completed distribution list and save it.

L2

4) Open the file called '**Joshua_Temple**'.

   a) Open a new contact window. Create a new contact for Joshua including all the details you've been given. Take a screen shot of the window and then save the contact.

   b) Open a new blank email. Address the email to the 'Team A' distribution list that you set up in Task 3. Cc the email to Joshua.

   c) Give the email the subject 'Team meeting' and paste in the email message text from the file '**Joshua_Temple**'.

   d) Take a screen shot of the completed email.

Organising your Inbox

Searching your Emails   EL3   L1   L2

1) You can **search** the emails in your inbox using the **search bar**.

2) Just **type** in the **word** (or words) you want to search for.

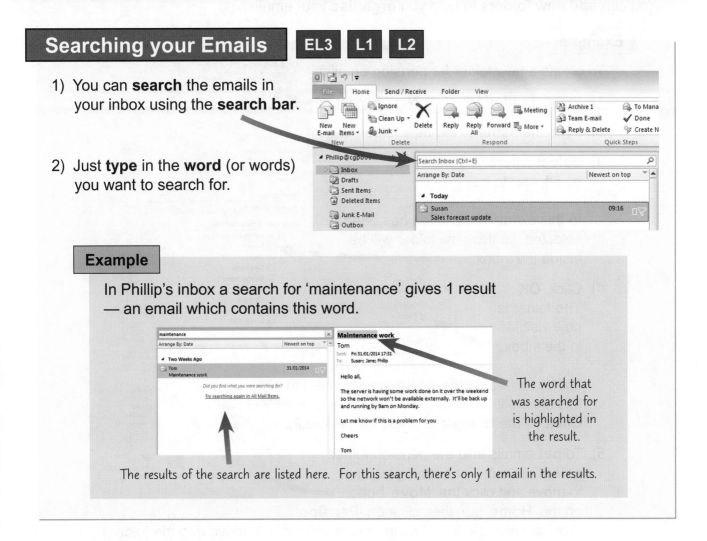

Example

In Phillip's inbox a search for 'maintenance' gives 1 result — an email which contains this word.

The word that was searched for is highlighted in the result.

The results of the search are listed here. For this search, there's only 1 email in the results.

Sorting Emails   L1   L2

In Outlook®, you can change the **order** that emails are **listed** in.
You can **sort** emails by their **date** (this is the most common way),
who **sent** them (the sender) and in lots of other ways.

Example

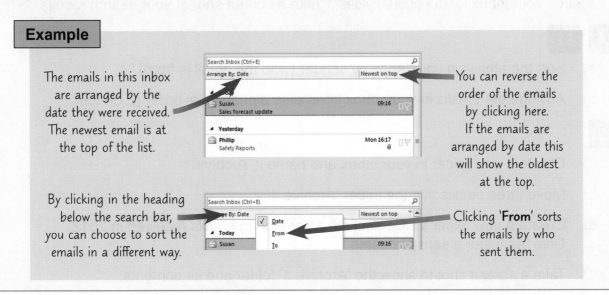

The emails in this inbox are arranged by the date they were received. The newest email is at the top of the list.

You can reverse the order of the emails by clicking here. If the emails are arranged by date this will show the oldest at the top.

By clicking in the heading below the search bar, you can choose to sort the emails in a different way.

Clicking 'From' sorts the emails by who sent them.

Organising Emails into Folders L2

You can **add new folders** to help you **organise** your emails.

Example

To create a new folder for pension emails:

1) In the '**Folder**' tab click '**New Folder**'.

2) Type the **name** of the new folder.

3) **Select where** you want the new folder to go.

   In this example the inbox has been selected, so this new folder will be inside the inbox.

4) Click '**OK**'. The folder is now visible in the inbox.

   If a folder has a **little white triangle** next to it, this means it has more folders inside it. **Click** on the **triangle** to show all the folders.

5) To **put** emails **into** the pension folder, **select** the email or emails you want to move and click the '**Move**' button on the '**Home**' tab, then click on '**Pension**'. (You can also **click** and **drag** emails you want to move into the folder.)

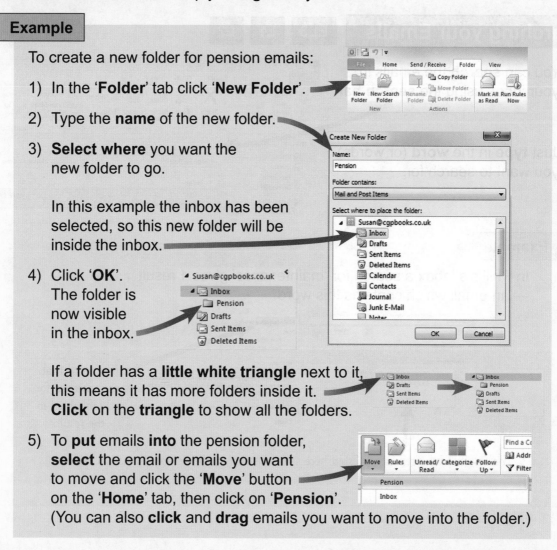

Practice Tasks

EL3 **L1** **L2**

1) Search your inbox for 'functional skills'. Take a screen shot of your search results.

L1 **L2**

2) a) Sort the emails in your inbox by sender (who the email is from).

   b) Arrange the emails in your inbox in reverse alphabetical order (Z on top).

L2

3) a) Create a new folder in your inbox and name it 'Archive 1'.

   b) Move three emails into the folder 'Archive 1'.

   c) Create a new folder inside 'Archive 1' for storing emails received in 2012. Give the folder a sensible name.

   d) Take a screen shot to show the 'Archive 1' folder and its contents.

Using and Writing Emails

Safety when Using Email　`EL3` `L1` `L2`

1) It's important to use email safely. If you're not careful you could **download viruses** or put your **personal information** at **risk**.

2) Emails can contain **viruses**. To reduce the chance of downloading a virus, you should only open **attachments** or click on **links** in emails sent from a **trustworthy source**.

Trustworthy sources include people that you know like friends and family.

3) **Never** open an attachment or click on a link sent from an **email address** that you **don't recognise**.

4) It's a good idea to have up to date **antivirus software** on your computer.

5) Some security software and email services also have **spam filters** — any emails that look like spam get put into a 'Junk' or 'Spam' folder.

Spam emails are emails that you haven't asked for or 'signed up' to receive. A lot of them are adverts.

 Junk E-Mail

6) Always keep the **password** you use to access your emails a **secret**. This stops someone else logging in to your email account and using it.

It's not a good idea to write your password down on paper — if someone finds it they could access your emails.

Don't Send Personal Information by Email　`EL3` `L1` `L2`

1) It's **not a good idea** to send important **personal information** (like your address and bank account details) by email.

2) The reason for this is that **email isn't 100% secure**. The information you send could be intercepted — someone other than the person you sent it to might be able to read it.

3) If you get an email asking for **lots of personal information**, be **suspicious**. The email might be from someone trying to steal your personal information.

4) It's worth remembering that whatever information you send in an email could be **forwarded on to someone else**. Have a think before you send private information.

Show Respect to Others in Emails　`EL3` `L1` `L2`

1) You should write emails so they are **polite** and **respectful** of other people.

2) You should write emails in the **same way** you'd write a letter.

3) In **formal emails** (see next page) make sure you use **proper language** — don't use 'text speak' or less formal language just because it's an email.

How to Write an Email L1 L2

You can use formal or informal writing in emails.

- **Formal writing** sounds **serious** and **professional**. A example of when you'd use this is when you're filling in a job application, or when you're at work.

- **Informal writing** sounds **chatty**. It's used when you're emailing friends and family.

Example

Here's an example of an email written in a **formal** way.

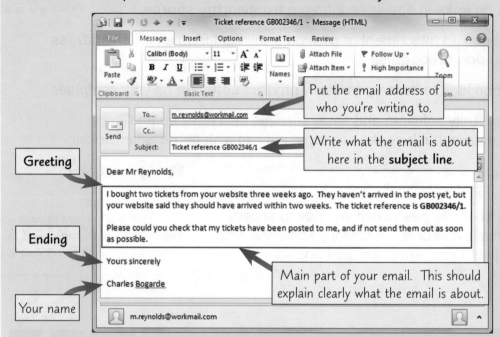

Subject line: This should give the person receiving the email an idea of what it's about before they read it.

Greeting: In a formal email this should start with 'Dear', followed by a title (for example Mr or Mrs) and the surname of the person. If you don't know the person's name you can use 'Dear Sir/Madam' instead. For an informal email you might use 'Hi' or 'Hello' and just the first name of a person.

Ending: You should end with 'Yours sincerely' if you know the name of the person you've emailed. Use 'Yours faithfully' if you don't know their name. In an informal email you might use 'See you soon' or 'Best wishes'.

Always end an email with your name. Give your full name in formal emails and just your first name in informal ones.

You can **format the text** in an email in lots of different ways using the buttons at the top of the window.

See page 47 for more information about formatting text.

It's a good idea to do a **spellcheck** before you send an email.
Click the '**Review**' tab and then '**Spelling & Grammar**' to do this.

There's more about spellchecking on page 48.

Practice Tasks

EL3 **L1** **L2**

1) Open a new blank email.

    a)   Address the email to jane@cgpbooks.co.uk.

    b)   Make the subject of the email 'Email security'.

    c)   Write an email to Jane that contains the answers to these questions:

        1. Why is it important to keep your email password a secret?

        2. Give one way that you can reduce the risk of getting computer viruses.

    d)   Take a screen shot of your completed email.

EL3 **L1** **L2**

2) Open a new blank email. In this task you're going to write an email to a friend.

    a)   Address the email to one of your contacts.
         If you don't have any contacts stored use susan@cgpbooks.co.uk.

    b)   Write an email to a friend asking them if they would like to come to a meeting about setting up a new sports club.
         Tell them that the meeting will be held next Wednesday at the cricket club. Don't forget to put a sensible subject line and to use a greeting and an ending on the email.

    c)   Take a screen shot of your completed email.

L1 **L2**

3) Open a new blank email. In this task you're going to write an email to a hotel manager.

    a)   Address the email to the hotel manager, Mrs Helen Wood.
         Her email address is helenwood@qualityservice.com.

    b)   Write an email to the manager asking to change a booking you've made. The booking was made for the 12th of December but you'd like to change it to the 18th of December. Ask her if this would be possible. Put the dates in **bold** in the email.

    c)   Run a spellcheck and take a screen shot of your completed email.

L1 **L2**

4) Open a new blank email. In this task you're going to email a washing machine company.

    a)   Address the email to the company. The email address is applianceparts@gmx.co.uk.

    b)   Write an email to the company asking how much it would cost to buy a washing machine part from them and have it delivered to you. The code for the part is B62370-2. Put the code in **bold** in the email.

    c)   Run a spellcheck and take a screen shot of your completed email.

Formatting Text

Word Processors are used to Change Text `EL3` `L1` `L2`

1) **Word processors** let you **change** how your text **looks**. This is called **formatting**.

2) They can do fancy things like **adding pictures** or **checking spelling** and **grammar**.

3) Word processors can be used to make things like **letters**, **leaflets**, **posters**, **flyers**...

4) One of the most common word processors is **Microsoft® Word®**, which is used here.

Example

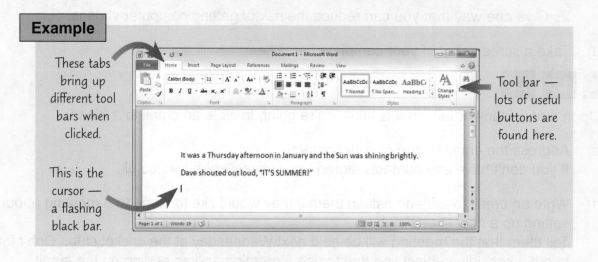

These tabs bring up different tool bars when clicked.

This is the cursor — a flashing black bar.

Tool bar — lots of useful buttons are found here.

It was a Thursday afternoon in January and the Sun was shining brightly.

Dave shouted out loud, "IT'S SUMMER!"

Entering Text `EL3` `L1` `L2`

1) To **enter** text, **click** anywhere on the page and **start typing**.

2) Use the **mouse** or **arrow keys** to **move** the **cursor** to a new place.

3) Press '**Enter**' or '**Return**' to move to a **new line**.

4) Use the '**Space Bar**' to make **spaces**. See page 5 for more on keyboard keys.

5) Use '**Shift**' or '**Caps Lock**' to get **capital letters**.

6) To get the **top symbol** on a key, hold '**Shift**' and press the key.

7) Press '**Delete**' or '**Backspace**' to **remove letters**, **numbers** or **symbols**.

8) To **select text**, **click** and **hold**, then drag from the **start** to the **end** of the text you want.

9) To **move text**, select it, then click on it and **drag** it to a new place.

10) You can also **add** text using a **text box**.

11) Click on the '**Text Box**' button on the '**Insert**' tab tool bar, then choose from the list.

Cut, Copy and Paste EL3 L1 L2

1) Use these **buttons** on the '**Home**' tool bar to **cut**, **copy** and **paste**.

2) **Select** the text you want to copy, then click '**Copy**'.

3) **Move** the cursor to where you want to put the text, then click '**Paste**'.

4) '**Cut**' works the same way as '**Copy**', but it **deletes** the original selected text too.

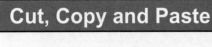

You can Change How the Text Looks EL3 L1 L2

To do this, **select** the text then use these **font buttons** on the '**Home**' toolbar:

Click this, then choose from the list to change the font (style of the text). E.g. Arial or Times New Roman.

Click this to change the size of the text. The larger the number, the larger the size.

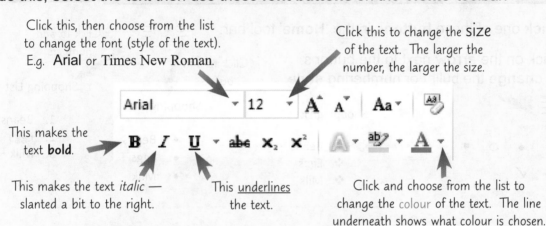

This makes the text **bold**.

This makes the text *italic* — slanted a bit to the right.

This <u>underlines</u> the text.

Click and choose from the list to change the colour of the text. The line underneath shows what colour is chosen.

If you change these **before typing**, everything typed **afterwards** will look that way.

Alignment EL3 L1 L2

1) There are **four different** ways to **align** text:

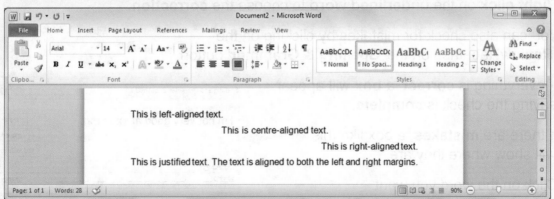

2) Use these **buttons** on the '**Home**' toolbar to **align** text **after** you've selected it:

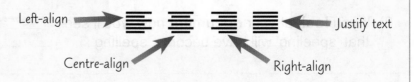

Left-align

Justify text

Centre-align

Right-align

Section Four — Word Processing

Line Spacing `EL3` `L1` `L2`

1) **Select** the text you want to **change**, then click this button in the '**Home**' toolbar.

2) Click on a **spacing** from the drop-down **menu**.

3) Line spacing is **usually** set at **1.15**.

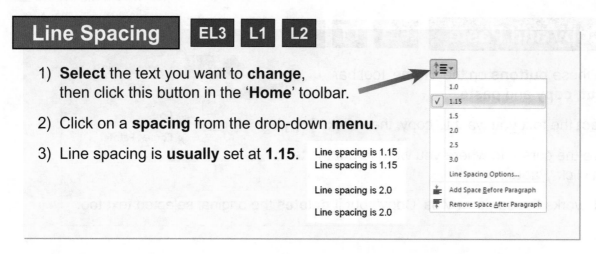

Line spacing is 1.15
Line spacing is 1.15

Line spacing is 2.0

Line spacing is 2.0

Bullet Points and Numbering are Good for Lists `EL3` `L1` `L2`

1) **Click** one of these **buttons** in the '**Home**' tool bar:

2) Click on the **arrow** next to the buttons to **change** the bullet or numbering **style**.

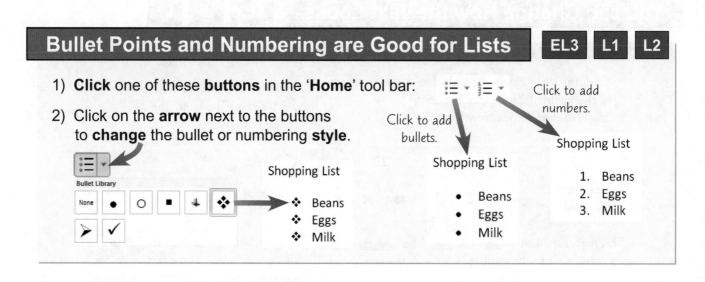

Click to add bullets.

Click to add numbers.

Shopping List
* Beans
* Eggs
* Milk

Shopping List
• Beans
• Eggs
• Milk

Shopping List
1. Beans
2. Eggs
3. Milk

Spellchecking `EL3` `L1` `L2`

1) Some word processors automatically **underline** spelling and grammar **mistakes**.

2) **Spelling** errors are often underlined in **red** and **grammar** errors in **green or blue**.

3) **Right click** on the **underlined word** to choose the **correction**.

4) You can also check for mistakes by clicking on the '**Review**' tab, then on the '**Spelling & Grammar**' button.

5) If everything is **correct**, a **box** will appear saying the check is **complete**.

6) If there are **mistakes**, a box like this will show where they are.

7) Click on the word you want to **replace** it with, then click '**Change**'.

8) If you **look** at your **document** now, you'll see that 'speeling' will have become 'spelling'.

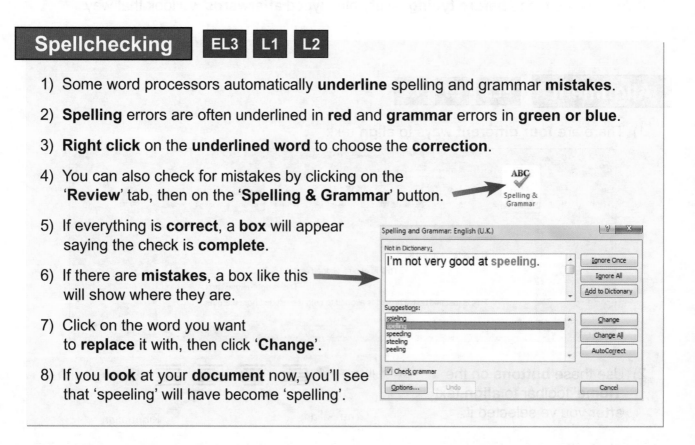

Practice Tasks

EL3 **L1** **L2**

1) Open a new word processing document.

   a) Enter the text as shown in the example Word® document on page 46.

   b) Save the file using a suitable name.

EL3 **L1** **L2**

2) Open the file called '**Amazon**'.

   a) Change the line spacing of all the text to 1.5.

   b) Right-align the date, and change its font to Times New Roman.

   c) Centre-align 'News of the Week' and change its size to 26.

   d) Add bullet points to: 'A purple passionflower with spaghetti-like petals,
   A monkey that purrs,
   A fingernail sized frog.'

   e) Make 'Article by Doris Smith' **bold** and *italic*.

   f) Correct the three spelling mistakes.

   g) Save the file using a suitable name.

EL3 **L1** **L2**

3) Open the file called '**Invitation1**'.

   a) Format the text to make it look as similar as you can to this invitation.

   b) Save the file using a suitable name and close the program.

Dave and Tania are getting hitched!

Dear friend

We're getting married on Saturday 14th July and we'd love you to come and celebrate with us.

Love is in the air

Where: St John's in the Valley, Cumbria

When: One o'clock

We want our wedding to be a really fun and relaxed day. The wedding reception is going to be in the church hall and we're going to have a bouncy castle and games to play outside. There'll be a barbecue and plenty of booze to go around. We'd like everyone to stay for the evening and dance their socks off.

Dress Code: Please come in whatever you feel most comfortable wearing. If you want to wear jeans, feel free.

Presents: We're going to Mauritius on our honeymoon. We'd be really grateful if you could contribute to our honeymoon fund. If you'd prefer not to, our favourite things are:

1. Ornaments
2. Gift vouchers
3. Chocolates

Please let us know if you can come by emailing *daveandtania@email.com*

Formatting Documents

Margins, Page Orientation and Size `EL3` `L1` `L2`

1) **Margins** are **gaps** without text at the **top**, **bottom** and **sides** of the page.

2) To change their **size**, click the '**Page Layout**' tab, then '**Margins**'.

3) Choose a **different** margin **size** by **clicking** on it.

4) Change the **orientation** by clicking the '**Page Layout**' tab, then this button.

5) Change the **size** of your page using the '**Size**' button also on the '**Page Layout**' tool bar.

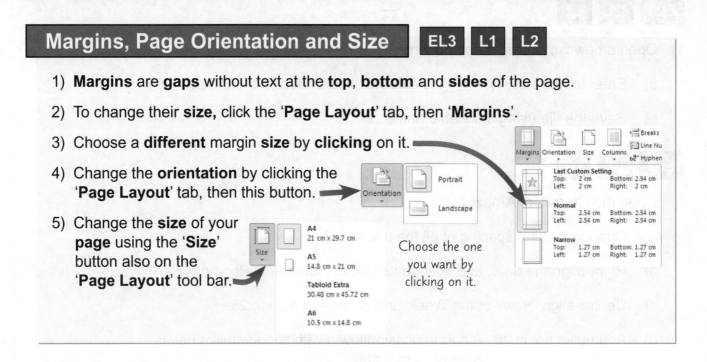

Choose the one you want by clicking on it.

Headers and Footers `EL3` `L1` `L2`

1) Use **headers** and **footers** to add **information** to **every page**. For example, your name.

2) **Headers** appear at the **top** of the page and **footers** appear at the **bottom**.

3) To add them to the page, click these **buttons** on the '**Insert**' tool bar:

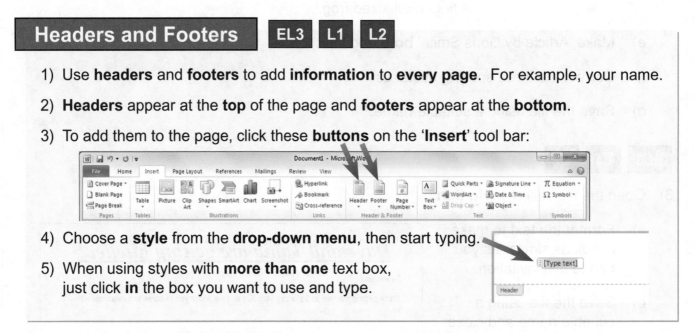

4) Choose a **style** from the **drop-down menu**, then start typing.

5) When using styles with **more than one** text box, just click **in** the box you want to use and type.

Page Numbers can be Added Automatically `EL3` `L1` `L2`

1) To **add page numbers** to every page click the '**Page Number**' button on the '**Insert**' tool bar.

2) Choose **where** the number will appear and its **style** by **clicking** on an option.

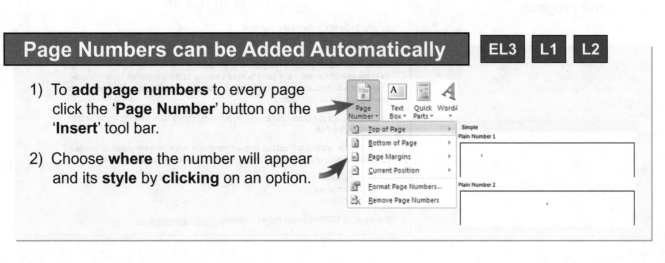

Page Borders can be Added to Every Page EL3 L1 L2

Click the '**Page Borders**' button on the '**Page Layout**' tool bar and this **box** will **appear**:

Choose a border style by clicking on an option.

Change the border colour here.

Change the border width here.

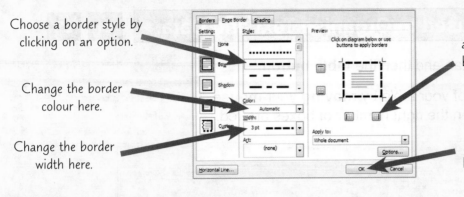

Click these buttons to add or remove the sides of borders. For example, this one changes the border at the right-hand side.

Click 'OK' when you're happy with the settings.

Printing EL3 L1 L2

Click the '**File**' tab, then click '**Print**' (on the left hand side).

Click this once you're happy with the choices below.

Click this to choose your printer.

Click this to change the orientation.

This lets you change the size of the margins.

This lets you print multiple pages per sheet.

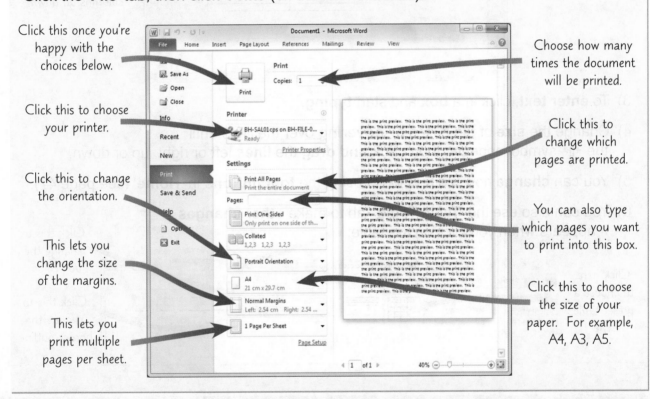

Choose how many times the document will be printed.

Click this to change which pages are printed.

You can also type which pages you want to print into this box.

Click this to choose the size of your paper. For example, A4, A3, A5.

Practice Task

EL3 L1 L2

1) Open the file called '**Invitation2**'.

   a) Set the orientation to Portrait and the margins to Normal.

   b) Add a border like this ▬▬▬ to the pages, with a thickness of 3 pt.

   c) Add a footer saying '14/07/14 - Be there or be square!'.

   d) Print the document so that there are 2 pages per sheet of paper.

   e) Save the file using a suitable name and close the program.

Tables

Tables can be used to Organise Text and Data `L1` `L2`

1) Click the 'Insert' tab and then the **table button**.

2) Choose the **size** of your table by **moving** your **mouse** and **clicking** when the right number of boxes are red.

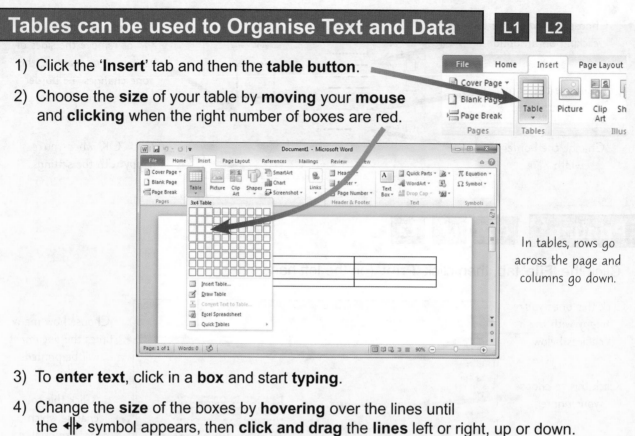

In tables, rows go across the page and columns go down.

3) To **enter text**, click in a **box** and start **typing**.

4) Change the **size** of the boxes by **hovering** over the lines until the ◄║► symbol appears, then **click and drag** the **lines** left or right, up or down.

5) You can **change** how the **text** looks using the **font buttons** in '**Home**' (see page 47).

6) You can also use the '**Table Tools**' tab to make **other changes**. It appears when you click on the table:

Click here to choose a preset table style.

Click this to change the box colour.

Click this to change the border outline.

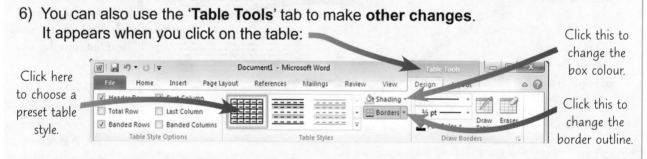

Practice Task

`L1` `L2`

1) Open the file called '**Gym**'.

   a) Insert a table under the 'Current fees' section. It should have column headings 'Age Range', 'Cost per Month' and 'Contract Length'.

   b) Fill in your table using the information from the 'Current fees' section.

   c) Make the text in the heading boxes bold. Colour in the heading boxes.

   d) Save the file using a suitable name.

Mail Merge

Mail Merge can Save you Loads of Time `L2`

1) **Mail merge** allows you **automatically add** data or information from **somewhere else** into a **word processing document**.

2) It's used to **create multiple documents** where only a **few details change** each time.

3) For example, a **company** might want to send out the **same letter** to all its customers, so just the **names and addresses** will need **changing** each time.

Example

Strongman Gym has asked you to send a letter out to all its customers under 30 years old. You can use mail merge to change the names and addresses automatically. Use this data (from another document):

Title	Surname	Address	Town	Postcode	Age	Account Number
Lord	Harrogate	13 Griffin Lane	Ambleside	LA19 4KR	67	1654684
Dr.	Little	35 River Road	Bowness	LA32 2HU	42	1654233
Mr.	Kyle	3 Stricklands Lane	Ambleside	LA32 4RD	28	1423659
Mrs.	Bean	14 Cooper Road	Kendal	LA30 3BL	46	1655542
Mr.	Atkinson	2 Nixon Lane	Kendal	LA30 3BH	25	1697546
Miss	Grainger	14 Park Drive	Bowness	LA32 2HY	27	1756459

1) First **write** the letter, leaving sensible **markers** for the information you'll merge.

(Title) (Surname)
(Address)
(Town)
(Postcode)

These are called 'markers'.

7th September 2014

Dear (Title) (Surname)

We are writing to inform you that some of the terms and conditions of your membership have changed. Please read the enclosed leaflet explaining these changes. If you require further information about these changes please contact us on 0215 695 777.

Bob Hollywood
Customer Service Manager

2) On the '**Mailings**' tab, click the '**Select Recipients**' button, then click '**Use Existing List**'.

3) Find and **select** the document containing the data you want and click '**Open**'.

4) If using a spreadsheet, select the **correct sheet** and click '**OK**'.

Data Source	☑	Surname ▾	Title ▾	Address ▾	Postcode ▾	Town ▾	Age ▾	Account Number ▾
Account_Nu...	☐	Harrogate	Lord	13 Griffin Lane	LA19 4KR	Ambleside	67	1654684
Account_Nu...	☐	Little	Dr.	35 River Road	LA32 2HU	Bowness	42	1654233
Account_Nu...	☑	Kyle	Mr.	3 Stricklands Lane	LA32 4RD	Ambleside	28	1423659
Account_Nu...	☐	Bean	Mrs.	14 Cooper Road	LA30 3BL	Kendal	46	1655542
Account...	☑	Atkinson	Mr.	2 Nixon Lane	LA30 3BH	Kendal	25	1697546
Account...	☑	Grainger	Miss	14 Park Drive	LA32 2HY	Bowness	27	1756459

5) Use the '**Edit Recipient List**' button to **choose** which data to **include** in the mail merge. You'll need to make sure everyone over 30 years old is unticked.

The merge fields look like this.

6) Select each **marker** and click '**Insert Merge Field**'. Choose the field you want to replace it with. Do this for **each piece** of **data**. For example, Title, Surname, Town.

7) If you **print** now, the printout will **show** the **merge fields**.

Example continues...

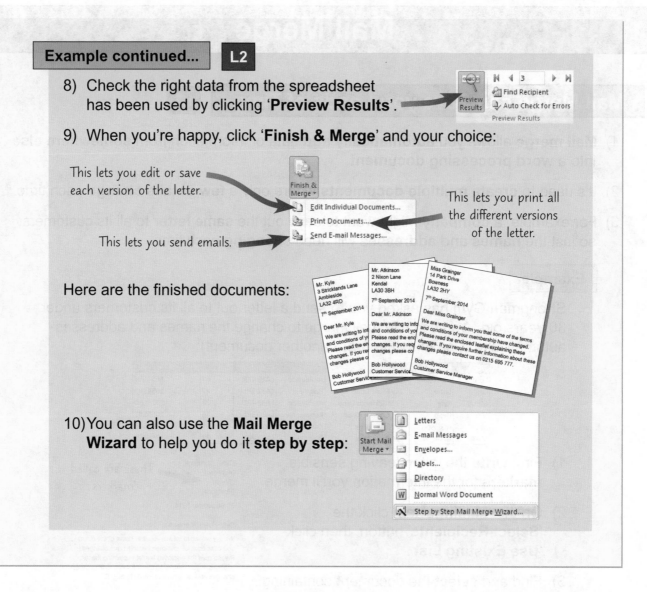

Example continued... L2

8) Check the right data from the spreadsheet has been used by clicking '**Preview Results**'.

9) When you're happy, click '**Finish & Merge**' and your choice:

This lets you edit or save each version of the letter.

This lets you print all the different versions of the letter.

This lets you send emails.

Here are the finished documents:

10) You can also use the **Mail Merge Wizard** to help you do it **step by step**:

Practice Tasks

L2

1) Open the file called '**Internet**'. Use mail merge to personalise the letters.

   a) Use 'Sheet1' of the file called '**Accounts**' as your recipient list.

   b) Replace the bracketed marker words with the appropriate merge fields.

   c) Print the merged letters.

L2

2) Open the file called '**Invoice**'.

   a) Use data from the file called '**Data**' and mail merge to produce invoices for only the customers who have paid.

   b) Print off these invoices.

Graphics

Inserting Graphics `EL3` `L1` `L2`

1) **Graphics** make documents look **nicer**.

2) To **add** a graphic to a word processor document click the 'Insert' tab and then the '**Picture**' button.

Graphics can be pictures, images, photos, maps, diagrams, logos...

3) A box will appear. Use this to **find** the graphic **file** you want to **add**:

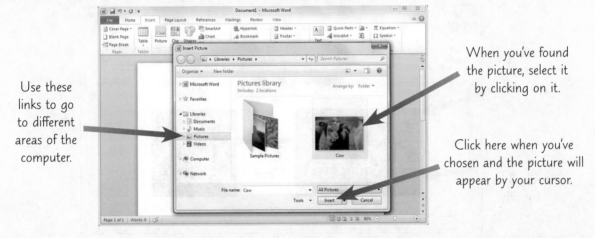

Use these links to go to different areas of the computer.

When you've found the picture, select it by clicking on it.

Click here when you've chosen and the picture will appear by your cursor.

4) You can also add graphics using the '**Copy**' and '**Paste**' buttons on the '**Home**' tool bar.

5) To **get rid** of a graphic, **click** on it and press '**Delete**' or '**Backspace**'.

Resizing and Rotating `EL3` `L1` `L2`

1) To **resize** a graphic, click on the **light blue points** around the sides and **drag**.

2) Use the **corner** circles to keep the graphic **in proportion**.

3) Using the **squares** on the **edge** will **stretch** and **distort** the graphic.

Click and drag to rotate.

Dragging the corners is the best way to resize images.

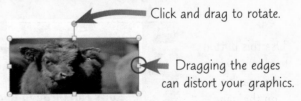

Dragging the edges can distort your graphics.

4) Graphics can be **rotated** by **dragging** the **green handle** above the image.

5) You can also use the '**Rotate**' button in the '**Picture Tools**' tab. **Click** on the **graphic** to open this tab.

6) You can **rotate** and **flip** graphics here too.

Click 'Rotate', then click on the option you want.

The picture has been flipped horizontally.

Cropping EL3 L1 L2

1) Graphics can also be **cropped** — this means **cutting** the **edges off** them.

2) Click on the graphic to bring up the '**Picture Tools**' tab, then click '**Crop**'.

Crop

3) Drag the **black handles** around to **select** an **area**.

4) Press the '**Crop**' button **again** to **cut** the graphic down.

Example

Crop the graphic so that the image is mainly of the cow.

Click and drag these handles.

The dark area will be cut off.

Click 'Crop'.

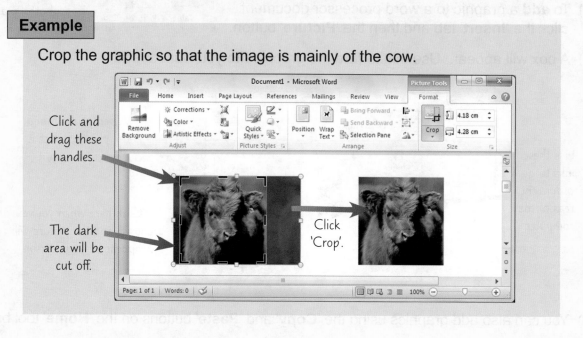

Positioning Graphics EL3 L1 L2

1) If the graphic is **added into** some **text**, you can change how the **text wraps** around it.

2) Click the '**Wrap Text**' button in the '**Picture Tools**' tool bar.

3) **Choose** a wrapping **style** from the drop down menu:

Use this button to change where the graphic is on the page.

To move the graphic to a different position, use this button again, or use 'Cut' and 'Paste', or click and drag.

These four options change how the text wraps around the graphic.

These two options put the graphic in front of or behind the text.

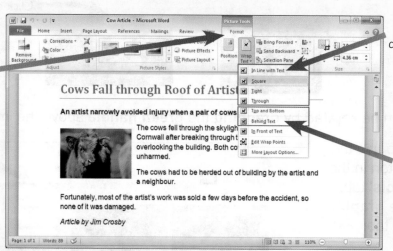

Adding Labels to Graphics   EL3   L1   L2

1) On the '**Insert**' tab, click '**Text Box**'.

Text Box ▾

2) Choose a **style**, or **draw your own** by clicking '**Draw Text Box**'.

3) **Click** on the page and **drag** to the correct size.

4) Start **typing** to enter text.

Change how the text looks by using the font buttons on the 'Home' tool bar (see page 47).

You can change how the text wraps around this box too (see previous page).

An artist narrowly avoided injury when a pair of cows fell through her roof.

The cows fell through the skylight of the workshop in Cornwall after breaking through the fence of a field overlooking the building. Both cows were said to be unharmed.

The cows had to be herded out of building by the artist and a neighbour.

The culprit

Fortunately, most of the artist's work was sold a few days before the accident, so none of it was damaged.

Article by Jim Crosby

5) To **remove** the **outline** of the box, click on it, then click '**Drawing Tools**', then '**Shape Outline**' and '**No Outline**'.

Clip Art and Image Galleries   EL3   L1   L2

1) Some word processors have built-in **image galleries**, often called **clip art galleries**.

2) You can also **buy** image galleries or **use** ones on the **internet**.

3) In Microsoft® Word®, click the '**Insert**' tab, then the '**Clip Art**' button.

4) A panel will open at the **right hand side** of the screen:

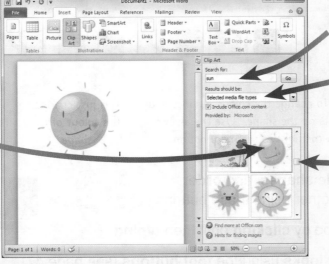

Type the keywords you want to search for in here, then click go.

This lets you choose the type of image you want. For example, illustrations (cartoons) or photographs.

When you find a graphic you like, double-click on it. Or click and drag it on to the page.

Scroll up and down to see the different images.

Choosing Graphics EL3 L1 L2

1) You need to use graphics that are **suitable** and **nice** to look at.

2) Think about the **purpose** of the document. For example, on a poster advertising trips to London, a picture of Buckingham Palace would be more suitable than a coach.

3) Think about the **audience**. For example, a leaflet aimed at **adults** should have more **grown-up** and **professional** looking graphics than one aimed at children.

Finding Graphics on the Internet EL3 L1 L2

1) You can use a **search engine** to find **graphics** on the **internet**.

2) Search for **keywords** connected to the graphics you want. See page 26 for more.

3) When you've found the one you want — **right-click**, click '**Copy**', then **paste** it straight into your document.

4) You can also click '**Save picture as...**' and **insert** the graphic as shown on p. 55.

Drawing Simple Graphics L1 L2

1) On the '**Insert**' tab, click '**Shapes**' and choose a **shape** from the drop-down menu.

2) **Click** and **drag** on the page to draw the shape.

3) **Click** on the shape to open the '**Drawing Tools**' tab:

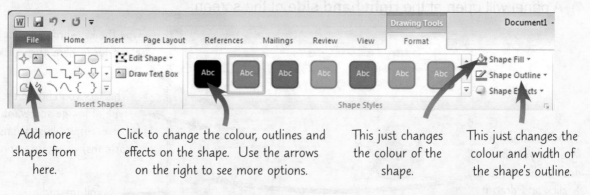

Add more shapes from here.

Click to change the colour, outlines and effects on the shape. Use the arrows on the right to see more options.

This just changes the colour of the shape.

This just changes the colour and width of the shape's outline.

4) You can draw **multiple shapes**, and **order them** on top of each other using these buttons: Bring Forward ▾ Send Backward ▾

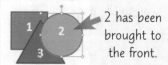 2 has been brought to the front.

5) **Enter text** into a shape by **clicking** on it then **typing**.

6) **Change** how the **text looks** using the **font buttons** (see page 47).

Practice Tasks

EL3 **L1** **L2**

1) Open the file called '**Gym_Leaflet**'.

   a) Using the boxes as a guide, choose three appropriate graphics from the second page.

   b) Insert the three graphics you've chosen into the gym leaflet on the first page.

   c) Save the file using a suitable name.

EL3 **L1** **L2**

2) Open the file called '**Diet**'.

   a) Crop the image to remove the blurred sections at the top and bottom.

   b) Flip the image horizontally.

   c) Add a label to your picture saying 'Examples of low GI foods.'

   d) Change the text wrapping of the image to square, then place it at the right hand side of the text below the 'Doctors recommend low sugar foods' heading.

   e) Save the file using a suitable name.

L1 **L2**

3) Open the file called '**Bike**'.

   a) Replace the blue boxes on page two with two suitable images from page one.

   b) Make sure the images are suitably formatted.

   c) Print out the finished voucher only (page two).

L1 **L2**

4) Julia has given you a sketch of a new logo.

   a) Create the logo using Julia's sketch as a guide.

   b) Save the file using a suitable name.

   c) Close the program.

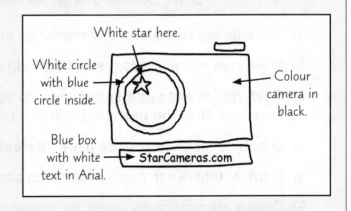

White star here.
White circle with blue circle inside.
Colour camera in black.
Blue box with white text in Arial. → StarCameras.com

Word Processing Tasks

Word Processors can be Used for Lots of Tasks   EL3 L1 L2

1) In the **test** you could be asked to make something with both text and graphics. For example, **posters**, **leaflets**, **invitations**, **receipts**, **newsletters**, **flyers** or **letters**.

2) You can use a **word processor program** to make these things.

3) Use the skills you've learned from this section to **edit** and **format** the document so it contains the **right information** and **looks nice**.

- **Read** the **questions carefully** and **follow** the **instructions** given.

- **Check** your **spelling** before printing or saving any documents.

- Think about the documents **purpose**. For example, a poster is used to **advertise** something, but a leaflet gives more information. Both need to be attractive but the poster should be **easier** and **quicker** to **read**.

- Think about the document's **audience**. For example, a letter to a customer should be **formal** and **professional** looking. A poster for children should be **informal**, **bright** and **cheerful**.

Use Formatting to Make Documents Look Nice   EL3 L1 L2

1) Use **different fonts** to make things **stand out**.

2) But **don't** use **more** than **three fonts** in one document — it will look **messy**.

3) Use **fonts** that are **easy to read** and **suitable** for the document.

> Times New Roman and Arial are good for formal documents.
> Comic Sans and Berlin Sans are nice, friendly fonts.

4) Use different **font sizes** to make things **stand out**. For example, titles.

5) Make sure you use a **font size** that's **big enough** to read **easily**.

6) **Bold**, *italics* and <u>underlining</u> can also be used to make things stand out. Don't use them **too much** or it will look **untidy**.

7) **Graphics** make things look more **interesting**.

8) **Maps** or **tables** can make information **easier** to **understand**.

9) **Colour** will make a document look nicer, but **don't** use **too much**.

10) Try using **borders**, different **text alignments** or **bullets** and **numbered lists** too.

Formal and Informal Documents EL3 L1 L2

Formal documents:

1) Use **fewer** and more **plain colours**.

2) Use **fewer font styles** and more **serious-looking** fonts.

3) Use **some formatting**, but it is usually kept **neat** and **simple**.

4) Often use **photos** instead of clip art or cartoons.

Informal documents:

1) Use **more** and **brighter colours**.

2) Use more **interesting** font **styles**.

3) Might include **clip art** or **cartoon graphics**, as well as **photos**.

Making a Poster   EL3 L1 L2

1) **Don't** add **too much detail** to posters — the **main** points should be **easy** to **find**.

2) They need to be **attractive**, so use **colours** and **graphics**.

3) The **text** needs to be **easy to read** from a **distance**.

Example

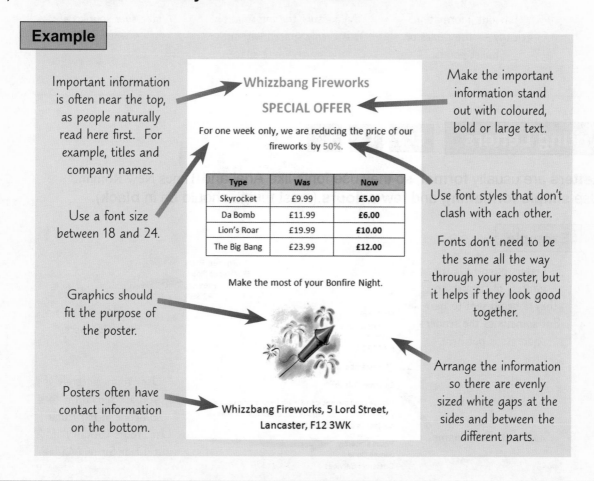

Making a Leaflet or Newsletter EL3 L1 L2

Leaflets and **newsletters** usually have **more detail** and **information** than posters.

Example

Break text up into clear, useful sections.

Choose suitable font sizes for text and headings. Try 18-24 for headings and 12-14 for text.

Make sure any graphics are suitable for the section they're in.

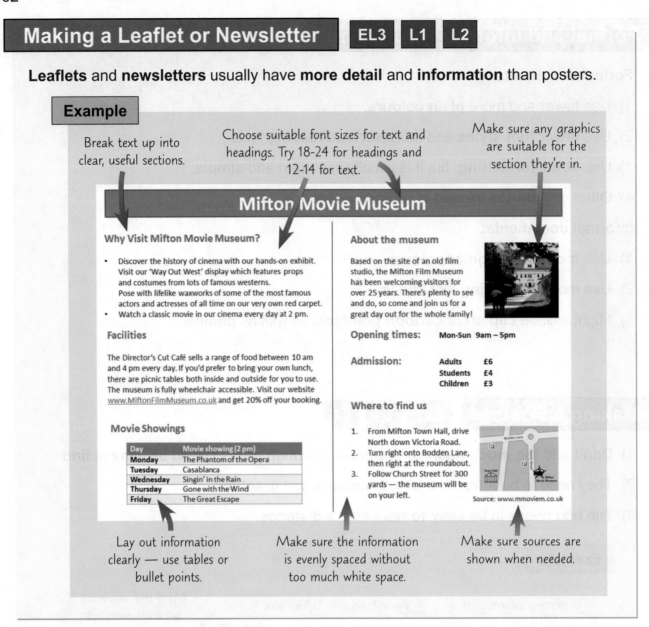

Mifton Movie Museum

Why Visit Mifton Movie Museum?

- Discover the history of cinema with our hands-on exhibit. Visit our 'Way Out West' display which features props and costumes from lots of famous westerns. Pose with lifelike waxworks of some of the most famous actors and actresses of all time on our very own red carpet.
- Watch a classic movie in our cinema every day at 2 pm.

Facilities

The Director's Cut Café sells a range of food between 10 am and 4 pm every day. If you'd prefer to bring your own lunch, there are picnic tables both inside and outside for you to use. The museum is fully wheelchair accessible. Visit our website www.MiftonFilmMuseum.co.uk and get 20% off your booking.

Movie Showings

Day	Movie showing (2 pm)
Monday	The Phantom of the Opera
Tuesday	Casablanca
Wednesday	Singin' in the Rain
Thursday	Gone with the Wind
Friday	The Great Escape

About the museum

Based on the site of an old film studio, the Mifton Film Museum has been welcoming visitors for over 25 years. There's plenty to see and do, so come and join us for a great day out for the whole family!

Opening times:	Mon-Sun	9am – 5pm

Admission:	Adults	£6
	Students	£4
	Children	£3

Where to find us

1. From Mifton Town Hall, drive North down Victoria Road.
2. Turn right onto Bodden Lane, then right at the roundabout.
3. Follow Church Street for 300 yards — the museum will be on your left.

Source: www.mmoviem.co.uk

Lay out information clearly — use tables or bullet points.

Make sure the information is evenly spaced without too much white space.

Make sure sources are shown when needed.

Writing Letters EL3 L1 L2

Letters are usually **formal**, so they use fonts like Arial and Times New Roman. Use **simple formatting** and **few colours** (most things should be in **black**).

Example

Letters often have the address of the person they're being sent to here. But sometimes the sender's address is put here.

They can have the date on them.

Start with Dear 'name'.

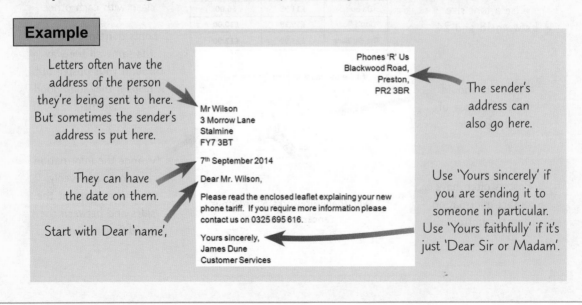

Phones 'R' Us
Blackwood Road,
Preston,
PR2 3BR

Mr Wilson
3 Morrow Lane
Stalmine
FY7 3BT

7th September 2014

Dear Mr. Wilson,

Please read the enclosed leaflet explaining your new phone tariff. If you require more information please contact us on 0325 695 616.

Yours sincerely,
James Dune
Customer Services

The sender's address can also go here.

Use 'Yours sincerely' if you are sending it to someone in particular. Use 'Yours faithfully' if it's just 'Dear Sir or Madam'.

Practice Tasks

EL3 **L1** **L2**

1) Create a poster to advertise the opening event for a new shop called 'Green Home'.

   a) Use the text from the file called '**Poster**'.

   b) Choose one graphic to include from the file called '**Poster**'.
   Insert it into a suitable place on your poster.

   c) Format the layout of the poster so that it looks nice and is suitable for purpose.
   Think about: font size, font style, colour, bullet points, borders, text alignment
   or any other type of formatting.

   d) Save the file with a suitable name.

L1 **L2**

2) Create a landscape A4 poster to advertise swimming lessons for children at
Mifton Leisure Centre. Use the plan below:

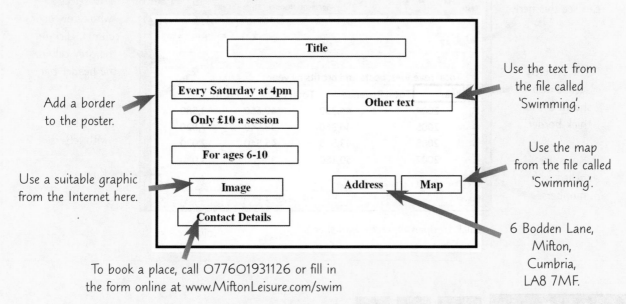

Format the poster so that it is attractive, accurate and suitable for the audience.
Print out the poster when you've finished.

L2

3) Create a leaflet advertising the Ram and Goat's Sunday Lunch.
Your leaflet must contain:

   a) The text from page one of the file called '**Pub**'.

   b) Graphics and text from page two of the file called '**Pub**'.
   (Follow the instructions on page two.)

   c) Format your leaflet so that it is attractive, accurate and suitable for the audience.

   d) Save the file using a suitable name.

Entering and Editing Data

Spreadsheets Organise Information   EL3   L1   L2

1) **Spreadsheets** hold lots of **data** and are useful for doing **calculations**.

2) **Microsoft® Excel®** is a common **spreadsheet** program and the one used here.

 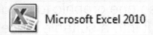
Microsoft Excel 2010

3) Each of the **little boxes** on a spreadsheet is called a **cell**.

4) Cells make up **rows** (lines **across** the page) and **columns** (lines **down** the page).

Example

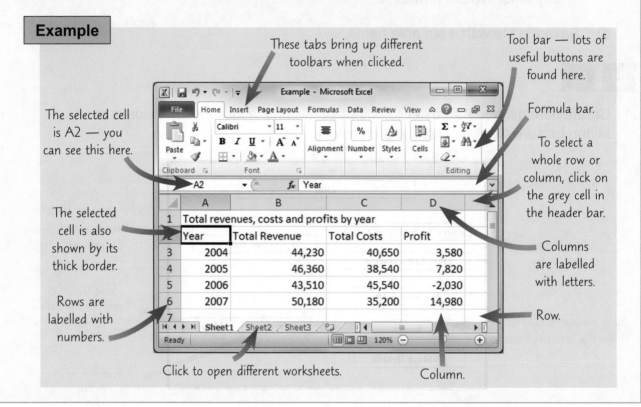

These tabs bring up different toolbars when clicked.

Tool bar — lots of useful buttons are found here.

The selected cell is A2 — you can see this here.

Formula bar.

To select a whole row or column, click on the grey cell in the header bar.

The selected cell is also shown by its thick border.

Columns are labelled with letters.

Rows are labelled with numbers.

Row.

Click to open different worksheets.

Column.

The spreadsheet shows:

	A	B	C	D
1	Total revenues, costs and profits by year			
2	Year	Total Revenue	Total Costs	Profit
3	2004	44,230	40,650	3,580
4	2005	46,360	38,540	7,820
5	2006	43,510	45,540	-2,030
6	2007	50,180	35,200	14,980
7				

Entering Data   EL3   L1   L2

1) To enter data, **click** on a cell and start **typing**.

2) To **edit** a cell's contents, click in the **formula bar** and make your change in the box.

3) Spreadsheets should have a **title** in the **first row** to explain what the data shows.

4) Each **column** should also be **labelled** in the second row.

5) **Extra information** can go in a **header** (at the top of the sheet) or **footer** (at the bottom). These only appear when you **print**. Click the 'Insert' tab and the 'Header & Footer' button to add them.

Some exam boards ask you to put your name as a footer on every printout.

6) To select **more than one** cell, click on one cell and **drag** the **cursor** over **all the cells** you want to **select**.

Header & Footer

Importing Data `L2`

1) Sometimes you might need to **import data** into a spreadsheet from **another file**.

2) This might be from a **text file** with the file extension '**.txt**'.

3) The data that goes into each cell will be **separated** somehow, often by **commas**.

Example

Import the revenue data from the 'Revenue' **text file** into a **spreadsheet**.

1) Open a new spreadsheet and click the '**From Text**' button on the '**Data**' tab.

2) Use the **window** that pops up to **find** the text file you want to import. When you find it, select it and click '**Import**'.

3) The data is separated by commas, so in the **box** that pops up (Text Import Wizard window step 1) make sure '**Delimited**' is selected and click '**Next**'.

Revenue - Notepad
File Edit Format View Help
Year, Total Revenue, Total Costs
2004, 44 230, 40 650
2005, 46 360, 38 540
2006, 43 510, 45 540
2007, 50 180, 35 200

4) In **step 2**, select '**Comma**' and click '**Next**'.

5) In **step 3**, select '**General**' and click '**Finish**'.

6) Finally, click on the cell in the spreadsheet where you want the **top left** cell of the imported data to go and click '**OK**'.

	A	B	C
1	Year	Total Revenue	Total Costs
2	2004	44 230	40 650
3	2005	46 360	38 540
4	2006	43 510	45 540
5	2007	50 180	35 200

A comma in the text file indicates a new cell in the row in the spreadsheet.

Different rows in the text file mean different rows in the spreadsheet.

Changing Row and Column Size `EL3` `L1` `L2`

1) You can **adjust** the **row height** or **column width** so your data **fits neatly** in the cells.

2) Hover over the **dividing line** on the **grey** column or row header bar until this **symbol** appears.

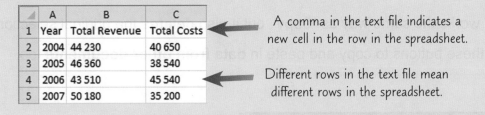

3) **Double-click** and the cell size will **automatically change** to **fit** your data.

4) Or **click and drag** left or right, or up or down until the cell is the **right size**.

5) You need to make sure all the data **fits neatly** into the cells before you **print**.

Insert or Delete Columns and Rows   EL3 L1 L2

1) To **add** a **column**, select the entire column to **the right** of where you want to add the new one.

2) Click the '**Insert**' button on the '**Home**' tab.

3) To add a **row**, select the entire row **below** where you want the new row and click '**Insert**'.

4) To **delete** a column or row, select the entire one and click the '**Delete**' button.

5) You can also **add or delete** them by **right-clicking** on a cell and selecting '**Insert...**' or '**Delete...**'.

Insert   Delete Format

Cells

Cut, Copy and Paste   EL3 L1 L2

1) Use these **buttons** on the '**Home**' tab to **cut**, **copy** and **paste**.

2) **Select** the text, cell or entire row or column you want to copy, then click '**Copy**'.

3) **Move** the cursor to where you want to put it, then press '**Paste**'.

4) '**Cut**' works the same way as 'Copy', but it also **deletes** the original selection.

5) Use these buttons to copy and paste in **data from other documents** too.

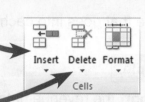

File   Home   Inse

Cut
Copy
Paste   Format Painter

Clipboard

Labelling Columns and Rows   EL3 L1 L2

Add **labels** to your columns or rows to make it **clear** what the data is about.

Example

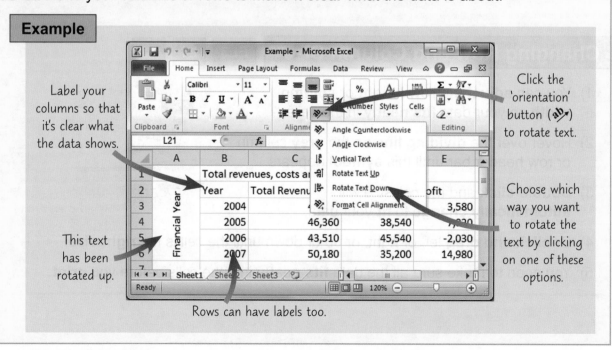

Label your columns so that it's clear what the data shows.

This text has been rotated up.

Rows can have labels too.

Click the 'orientation' button (⟋) to rotate text.

Choose which way you want to rotate the text by clicking on one of these options.

Practice Tasks

EL3 **L1** **L2**

1) Make sure you are sitting correctly at your desk and
   turn on your computer. Open the file called '**Gino**'.

   a)   Write your name in cell A1. Adjust the width so it displays correctly.

   b)   Go to cell C5 and change 2.75 to 2.00.

   c)   In row 6, change 'Orange juice' to 'Apple juice' in the 'Drink' column.

   d)   Save the file using a suitable name.

EL3 **L1** **L2**

2) Open the file called '**Luxury**'.

   a)   Insert a new column to the left of the column for 'Hotel Costs (£)'.
        Name this new column 'Restaurant Costs (£)' and make it display correctly.

   b)   Rotate the text 'Costs per year' up.

   c)   Add a footer and write your name in it.

   d)   Delete the row that contains the cell named 'Gas'.

   e)   Insert the following information in the 'Restaurant Costs' column:

Electricity	2739.45
Water	1695.12
Council Tax	2075
Wages	58625.21

   f)   Save the file using a suitable name and close the program.

L2

3) Open a new spreadsheet file.

   a)   Import the data from the text file '**Letting**' into your spreadsheet.

   b)   Delete column D and insert a new column with the following data in it.

Property	12 Beville Street
Number of Bedrooms	3
Rent per Month (£)	660
Deposit (£)	660
Furnished	No

   c)   Make sure all the data is clear and easy to read.

   d)   Save the file using a suitable name and close the program.

Formatting Spreadsheets

Make Information Stand Out   EL3 L1 L2

To do this, **select** the cell then use these **font buttons** on the '**Home**' tab:

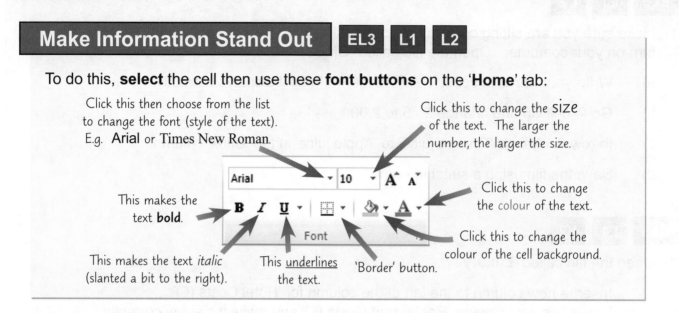

Click this then choose from the list to change the font (style of the text). E.g. Arial or Times New Roman.

Click this to change the size of the text. The larger the number, the larger the size.

This makes the text **bold**.

Click this to change the colour of the text.

This makes the text *italic* (slanted a bit to the right).

This underlines the text.

'Border' button.

Click this to change the colour of the cell background.

Add Borders to Cells to Make them Stand Out   EL3 L1 L2

1) To give a cell a **border**, select a cell then **click** the '**Border**' button on the '**Home**' tab.

2) Click on the arrow to choose what **type of border** you want.

3) You can change the border of **several cells** at a time by **selecting them all** and choosing the border you want.

4) **Gridlines** are the **grey outlines** around the cells.

5) To turn them on and off, go to the '**Page Layout**' tab and tick or untick the '**Print**' and '**View**' boxes in the '**Gridlines**' section.

Borders

- Bottom Border
- Top Border
- Left Border
- Right Border

Merge and Unmerge Cells   EL3 L1 L2

1) **Merging** cells means **joining** a number of cells into a **single** cell.

2) **Select** all the cells you want to merge and then **click** the '**Merge & Center**' button.

3) To **unmerge** the cells, **select** the merged cell and click the button again.

Example

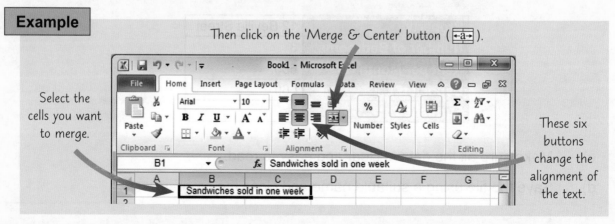

Then click on the 'Merge & Center' button ( ).

Select the cells you want to merge.

These six buttons change the alignment of the text.

Format the Numbers in a Cell EL3 L1 L2

1) You can **change** the way numbers **appear** in a cell.

2) For example, you can change numbers into **currency** format
   so they have a '**£**' sign and **two decimal places.**

3) **Select** the cell or cells you want to format and
   use these buttons on the '**Home**' tab:

Shows you what
the formatting is for
the cell selected.

Click the arrow to change the format.
Choose the type of formatting from the
drop-down menu. For example, currency.

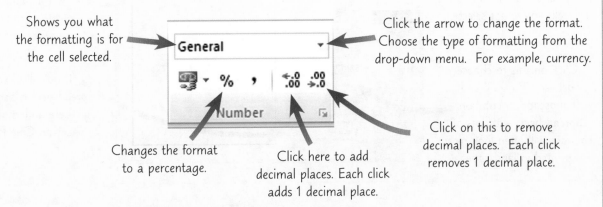

General

Number

Changes the format
to a percentage.

Click here to add
decimal places. Each click
adds 1 decimal place.

Click on this to remove
decimal places. Each click
removes 1 decimal place.

4) If you're asked in an exam to **format** the spreadsheet and
   make information **clear** and **easy to read** it usually means:

   • Format the cells so **currency**, **number** or other formats are used.

   • Adjust the **column and row size** so everything can be **read easily** (see p. 65).

   • Make important information **stand out** (see p. 68).

Examples of Numerical Formatting EL3 L1 L2

These are the most common types of formatting you will need:

1) **Number** — For **normal numerical** data. For example, the number
   of cars sold. You can change the number of **decimal places** in this format.
   For example, if you choose 1 decimal place and type 5 it will turn into 5.0.

2) **Currency** — For when the data is **money** or **prices**. It adds a **£** and
   two decimal places. For example, if you type 3.5 it will turn into £3.50.

3) **Date** — Lets you choose a **format** for a **date**.
   For example, you can choose 14/03/2014 or 14 March 2014.

4) **Percentage** — **Multiplies** the cell value by **100** and adds a % symbol.
   For example, if you type 0.1 it will become 10%.

Printing a Spreadsheet EL3 L1 L2

To **print** your spreadsheet click on the '**File**' tab and click '**Print**' (on the left-hand side).

Click on this to choose what from the spreadsheet to print. 'Print Active Sheets' will print the whole spreadsheet. 'Print Selection' will only print the cells you've got selected.

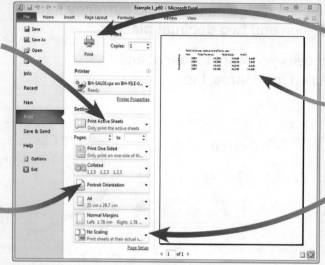

Click this to print.

This 'Print Preview' shows what will actually come out the printer.

Click on this to choose between 'Portrait' and 'Landscape' orientation. Spreadsheets with lots of columns will often look nicer printed in landscape.

If not all of your spreadsheet is showing, click here and choose 'Fit Sheet on One Page'.

Practice Tasks

EL3 L1 L2

1) Open the file called '**Bridgeshire**'.

   a)   Write your name in cell C10.

   b)   Merge cells B1 and C1 so the title is in a single cell.

   c)   Colour the merged cell yellow and bold the text to make it stand out.

   d)   Colour the cells B3 to B6 pale blue.

   e)   Add a border around all the whole spreadsheet.

   f)   Format cells C3 to C6 so that they are 'currency' cells and have two decimal places.

   g)   Print the spreadsheet out, with all the data showing clearly, in Landscape orientation.

L1 L2

2) Open the file called '**Leekton**'.

   a)   Merge cells B1-F1 and format them so that the title stands out.

   b)   Format the price data on the spreadsheet correctly

   c)   Make sure the spreadsheet is clear and easy to read.

   d)   Save the file using a suitable name.

Formulas

Formulas are Used to do Calculations   L2

1) You can make a spreadsheet **do maths** by adding in **formulas**.

2) Click the cell where the answer will go and **type the formula** into the **formula bar**.

3) All formulas **start** with an **=** sign.

4) Use cell letter and number **references** to tell the spreadsheet which **cells to use**. For example, **B4** or **C9**.

5) Use these **signs** to complete the formulas:

   + to add together numbers

   - to subtract numbers

   / to divide numbers

   ***** to multiply numbers

   If you type =B4+B5, then the spreadsheet will add the number in B4 to the number in B5.

   If you type =B4*B5, then the spreadsheet will multiply the number in B4 by the number in B5.

6) When you've typed in the formula, press **return** and the answer will **appear** in the **cell**.

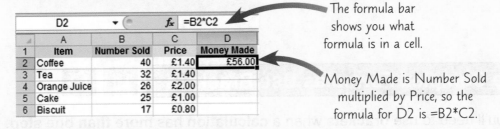

The formula bar shows you what formula is in a cell.

Money Made is Number Sold multiplied by Price, so the formula for D2 is =B2*C2.

7) Remember to put the answer cell in a **sensible** place. Just to the **right** or **underneath** the **cells used** is often the best place.

Copying Formulas   EL3   L1   L2

1) **Select** the cell with the formula in, then **copy and paste** it into another cell.

2) Or **click** on the cell and **hover** over the **bottom right corner** until you see this appear . Then **click and drag** over the other cells.

3) The spreadsheet will **automatically change** the **cell references** in the formula.

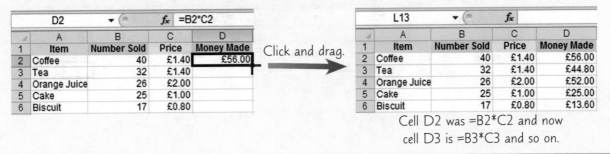

Click and drag.

Cell D2 was =B2*C2 and now cell D3 is =B3*C3 and so on.

AutoSum is Useful for Finding Total Amounts `EL3` `L1` `L2`

1) A function is a **formula** which comes already set up in a spreadsheet program. (Sum is a function. AutoSum is a group of functions grouped together.)

2) To quickly **add** together **lots of cells**, use the '**AutoSum**' button.

3) **Select** the cell you want the **answer** in.

4) Press the '**AutoSum**' button on the '**Home**' toolbar.

5) The cells being **added together** will be **automatically** selected.

6) If you need to **change the cells** selected, hover over the corner of the **blue highlighting** and when ↗ appears, **click and drag**.

7) If they're the cells you want to add, press '**Return**' and the **answer** will appear.

8) You can also type the AutoSum formula **directly** into a cell yourself: =SUM(U2:U6)

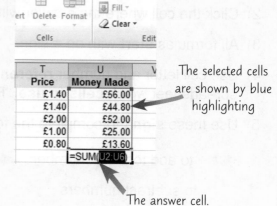

AutoSum button.

The selected cells are shown by blue highlighting

The answer cell.

Cell to start on.   Cell to finish on.

More Complex Formulas Use Brackets `L1` `L2`

1) You'll need to use **brackets** when a **calculation** has **more than one step**.

2) The brackets tell the program which step **comes first**.

Example

Add a **formula** to work out the **average** number of jobs per month. The average is the **total** number of jobs **divided** by the **number of months**.

1) This calculation has **two steps** so we need brackets.

2) The **first step** is finding the **total** number of jobs. This is (B2+C2+D2+E2).

3) The **second step** is **dividing** by the **number of months**, which is **4**. So the formula we need is =(B2+C2+D2+E2)/4.

You can also use the Average function — see page 74.

F2		f_x =(B2+C2+D2+E2)/4				
	A	B	C	D	E	F
1		January	February	March	April	Average
2	Number of Jobs	10	14	8	17	12.25

Printing with Formulas Showing   L1   L2

1) In the exam you might be asked to **print a spreadsheet** with the **formulas showing**.

2) Select the '**Formulas**' tab and then click '**Show Formulas**'.

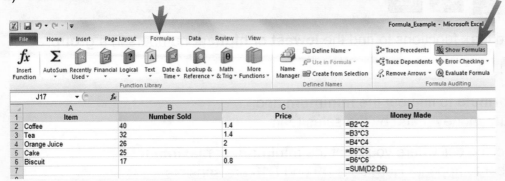

Adjust the column widths to make sure the formulas show properly (see p 65).

3) Instead of the **data** you calculated, the **formulas show** in the **cells**.

4) If you **print** the spreadsheet now, these **formulas** will **print** out.

5) To get the **data** to show (and print) again, click on '**Show Formulas**' again.

Practice Tasks

EL3   L1   L2

1) Open the file called '**Wash**'.

   a)   Find the total number of cars washed over the week by entering the formula =SUM(B2:B8) into cell B9.

   b)   Enter a suitable formula into cell D2 to find the money made by the car wash on Monday. [Money made = number of cars washed x price].

   c)   Copy the formula from cell D2 into all the cells down to and including D8.

   d)   Enter a suitable formula into cell D9 to calculate the total money made by the car wash over the week.

   e)   Save the file using a suitable name.

L1   L2

2) Open the file called '**Loan**'.

   a)   Use a formula to work out the amount still owed by each customer.

   b)   Use a formula to work out the totals for each column.

   c)   Make the name of the customer who owes the most stand out.

   d)   Produce a printout of the finished spreadsheet with the formulas showing.

   e)   Save the file using a suitable name.

More Formulas and Functions

Min and Max L1 L2

Use the **Min** and **Max** functions to find the **lowest** or **highest** numbers in a **group**.

Example

Use a **formula** to find out the **minimum** and **maximum** money made by the sales team.

1) Select the cell where you want the **minimum** or **maximum** number to appear. Here cells **D9** and **D10** are sensible.

2) Click the **arrow** next to '**AutoSum**' and pick '**Min**' or '**Max**' from the list.

3) Make sure all the **cells** you're **interested** in are **selected**. Here it's **D3** to **D8**.

4) Press '**Return**' and the answer should appear.

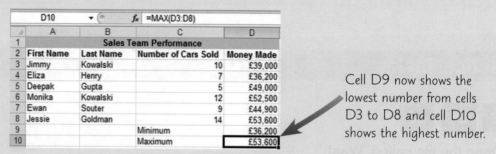

Cell D9 now shows the lowest number from cells D3 to D8 and cell D10 shows the highest number.

5) You can also type the formulas **directly** into a cell. For example '=MAX(D3:D8)' or '=MIN(D3:D8)'.

Average L1 L2

1) There is a function to calculate the **average** from a set of numbers.

2) **Click** the **arrow** next to the '**AutoSum**' button and choose '**Average**'.

3) Make sure all the **cells** you're **interested** in are **selected**. (Below it's **D3** to **D8**.)

4) Press '**Return**' and the answer should appear.

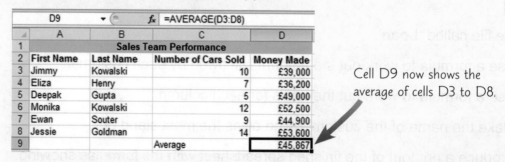

Cell D9 now shows the average of cells D3 to D8.

5) You can also type the formula **directly** into a cell. For example '=AVERAGE(D3:D8)'.

Median and Mode   L2

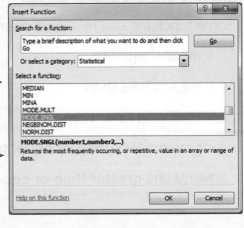

1) The **median** is the **middle number** when a **group of numbers** are put in order of **size**.

2) The **mode** is the **most common** number in a **group**.

3) Click the **arrow** next to the '**AutoSum**' button and choose '**More Functions**'.

4) This box will appear:

5) Select the category '**Statistical**' and choose '**MEDIAN**' or '**MODE.SNGL**' from the menu.

6) Another box will appear asking you to **enter** the cells you want to use. **Select** the cells you want to use and press '**OK**'.

7) You can also type the formulas **directly** into a cell. For example '=MEDIAN(B3:J3)' or '=MODE.SNGL(B3:J3)'.

Absolute or Relative Cell References   L2

1) Spreadsheets will **automatically** change **cell references** when formulas are **copied**.

2) This is called **relative cell referencing**.

3) Sometimes you **don't** want this to happen though, so you need to use **absolute cell referencing**.

4) Put a **dollar sign** before the letter and number of the cell reference you don't want to change. For example, A1.

You can make just a column or row absolute. Only put the dollar sign in front of that part. For example, $A1 would keep column A absolute but the row relative.

Example

The manager offered a special discount of £25.00 off each bill. Add a formula to cells C3 to C8 to show the new bill.

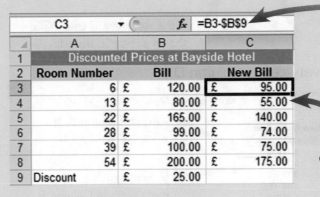

The discount is the same for every room number. So use an absolute cell reference — B9 would be typed in as B9 in the formula.

When you copy the formula into the other cells the B9 reference will stay put. For example, C4 will be =B4-B9.

Relational Operators L2

Some functions use relational operators:

= means **equal to**.

< means **less than**.

> means **greater than**.

<= means **less than or equal to**.

>= means **greater than or equal to**.

Examples

1) 3<7 means 3 is less than 7.

2) 10>5 means 10 is greater than 5.

3) z<=23 means z is less than or equal to 23.

The IF Function Can Make Words Appear Automatically L2

1) The **IF** function is used to show if a statement is **true or false**.

2) If the statement is **true**, you can make **one thing** appear in a **cell**.

3) If it's **false**, you can make **something else** appear.

4) What you make appear could be **words**, **numbers** or another **calculation**.

5) An IF formula is laid out like this:
=IF('statement','what happens if true',what happens if false').

6) If what appears is **words** then they have to have **quotation marks** around them, like "YES".

7) There should be **commas** between the **statement**, what happens if **true** and what happens if **false,** but **no spaces**.

Example

Sophie has been testing new coffee beans in her shop. If a type of bean got **50 or more** votes, she'd like '**YES**' to appear in Column D.

1) Select cell **D3** to type the **formula** in.

2) The formula should be =IF(B3>=50,"YES","NO").

If the statement is false, 'NO' should appear in the cell.

The statement is 'The value of cell B3 is greater than or equal to 50'.

If the statement is true, 'YES' should appear in the cell.

3) **Copy** the formula into every cell in Column D.

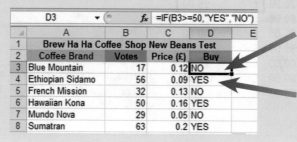

When there are 49 or less votes in Column B, the word No will appear.

When there are 50 or more votes in Column B, the word YES will appear.

AND, OR and NOT L2

1) You can use **AND**, **OR** and **NOT** as part of an IF function too.

>   **AND** — If the statement has **two parts** that **both** need to be true.
>
>   **OR** — If the statement has **two parts** but **only one** needs to be true.
>
>   **NOT** — When you need to show if something **isn't** true.

Example

Sophie now wants '**YES**' to appear in Column D **only** if the type of bean got 50 or more votes **and** the price is **less than or equal to** £0.18.

1) The **formula** should be =IF(AND(B3>=50,C3<=0.18),"YES","NO").

2) 'AND(B3>=50,C3<=0.18)' means 'B3 is greater than or equal to 50 **and** C3 is less than or equal to 0.18'.

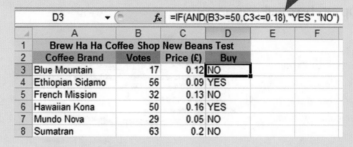

	A	B	C	D	E	F
	D3		f_x =IF(AND(B3>=50,C3<=0.18),"YES","NO")			
1	Brew Ha Ha Coffee Shop New Beans Test					
2	Coffee Brand	Votes	Price (£)	Buy		
3	Blue Mountain	17	0.12	NO		
4	Ethiopian Sidamo	56	0.09	YES		
5	French Mission	32	0.13	NO		
6	Hawaiian Kona	50	0.16	YES		
7	Mundo Nova	29	0.05	NO		
8	Sumatran	63	0.2	NO		

2) You'd use the **OR** or **NOT** function in a similar way.

3) For example, using =IF(OR(B3>=50,C3<=0.12),"YES","NO") would give 'YES' if B3 was greater than or equal to 50 **or** if C3 was less than or equal to 0.12.

Practice Tasks

 L1 L2

1) Open the file called '**Phones**'.

   a)   Find the minimum, maximum and average of the data provided.

   b)   Save the file using a suitable name.

L2

2) Open the file called '**Holidays**'.

   a)   Use absolute referencing to fill in the 'Hours Left' column.

   b)   For any employees with 7.5 or more hours left make the word 'Yes' appear in the 'Days Left' column. For others, make 'No' appear.

   c)   Produce a printout of the finished spreadsheet with the formulas showing.

   d)   Save the file using a suitable name.

Sorting and Filtering Data

Sorting Data `L1` `L2`

1) You can **sort data** so it's in **ascending** or **descending** order.

2) **Ascending** means numbers go **smallest to largest** or words go alphabetically **A-Z**.

3) **Descending** means numbers go **largest to smallest** or words go alphabetically **Z-A**.

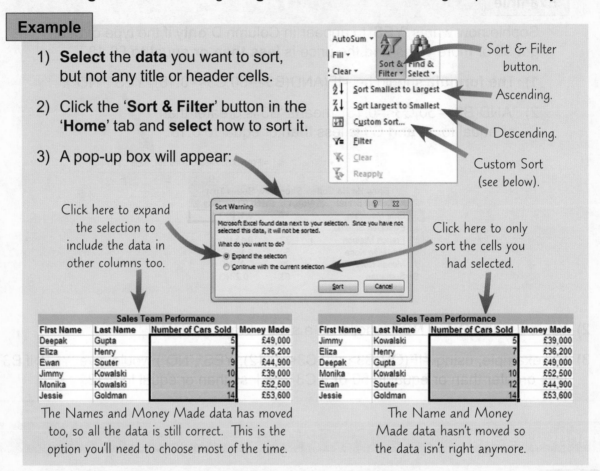

Example

1) **Select** the **data** you want to sort, but not any title or header cells.

2) Click the '**Sort & Filter**' button in the '**Home**' tab and **select** how to sort it.

3) A pop-up box will appear:

Sort & Filter button.

Ascending.

Descending.

Custom Sort (see below).

Click here to expand the selection to include the data in other columns too.

Sort Warning

Microsoft Excel found data next to your selection. Since you have not selected this data, it will not be sorted.

What do you want to do?
- Expand the selection
- Continue with the current selection

Click here to only sort the cells you had selected.

Sales Team Performance

First Name	Last Name	Number of Cars Sold	Money Made
Deepak	Gupta	5	£49,000
Eliza	Henry	7	£36,200
Ewan	Souter	9	£44,900
Jimmy	Kowalski	10	£39,000
Monika	Kowalski	12	£52,500
Jessie	Goldman	14	£53,600

The Names and Money Made data has moved too, so all the data is still correct. This is the option you'll need to choose most of the time.

Sales Team Performance

First Name	Last Name	Number of Cars Sold	Money Made
Jimmy	Kowalski	5	£39,000
Eliza	Henry	7	£36,200
Deepak	Gupta	9	£49,000
Monika	Kowalski	10	£52,500
Ewan	Souter	12	£44,900
Jessie	Goldman	14	£53,600

The Name and Money Made data hasn't moved so the data isn't right anymore.

4) Sometimes you'll need to **sort data** on more than one level. For example, by **name** and by **age**.

5) Select **all the data** on the spreadsheet this time, including **headers** but not titles.

6) Click '**Sort & Filter**' and then '**Custom Sort**'.

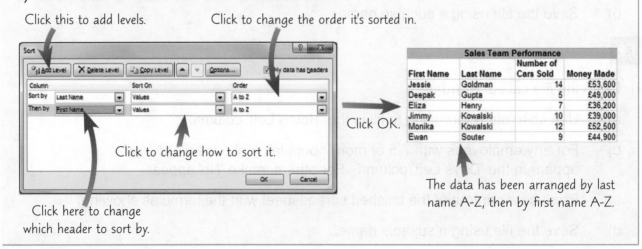

Click this to add levels.

Click to change the order it's sorted in.

Sort

Column	Sort On	Order
Sort by Last Name	Values	A to Z
Then by First Name	Values	A to Z

My data has headers

Click to change how to sort it.

Click here to change which header to sort by.

Click OK.

Sales Team Performance

First Name	Last Name	Number of Cars Sold	Money Made
Jessie	Goldman	14	£53,600
Deepak	Gupta	5	£49,000
Eliza	Henry	7	£36,200
Jimmy	Kowalski	10	£39,000
Monika	Kowalski	12	£52,500
Ewan	Souter	9	£44,900

The data has been arranged by last name A-Z, then by first name A-Z.

Filtering Data **L1** **L2**

You can add **filters** so **only data** that **matches** certain **criteria** (rules) can be **seen**.

Example

Filter the data so only people who've made **£45,000 or more** are shown.

1) **Select** the data you want to filter, including **headers**.

2) In the '**Home**' tab, click '**Sort & Filter**' and then '**Filter**'.

Add filter criteria (rules) by clicking here.

This drop-down menu shows the criteria options.

3) An **arrow** will appear in the **header box** of the data you selected.

4) Click on this arrow to bring up this.

5) Either **untick** the data you don't want...

6) ...Or choose '**Greater Than Or Equal To...**' as your criteria.

7) In the box that appears, **enter** or **select** a value here.

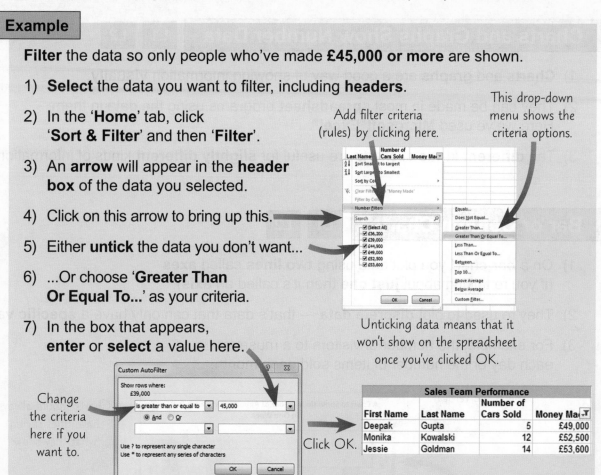

Unticking data means that it won't show on the spreadsheet once you've clicked OK.

Change the criteria here if you want to.

Click OK.

Sales Team Performance			
First Name	**Last Name**	**Number of Cars Sold**	**Money Ma**
Deepak	Gupta	5	£49,000
Monika	Kowalski	12	£52,500
Jessie	Goldman	14	£53,600

Practice Tasks

L1 **L2**

1) Open the file called '**Sales**'.

   a)   Sort the data in column B so that the sales team members are displayed in the order of highest sales to lowest sales.

   b)   Filter the data so that only sales team members with sales of £80,000 or more are shown on the spreadsheet.

   c)   Print out a copy of the sorted and filtered data on the spreadsheet.

   d)   Save the file using a suitable name.

L1 **L2**

2) Open the file called '**Interview**'.

   a)   Sort the data in ascending order of 'Written Test Score' within ascending order of 'Years of Experience'.

   b)   Save the file using a suitable name.

Types of Chart and Graph

Charts and Graphs Show Number Data `L1` `L2`

1) **Charts** and **graphs** are a good way of showing information **visually**.

2) They can be made in most **spreadsheet** programs using the data in them. Here we've used **Microsoft®Excel®**.

3) The **different kinds** of charts are useful for **slightly different** kinds of information.

Bar or Column Charts `L1` `L2`

1) On a **bar chart** you plot data using **two lines** called **axes** (if you're talking about **just one** then it's called an **axis**).

2) They're used to plot **discrete data** — that's data that can only have a **specific value**.

3) For example, the number of visitors to a museum each day or the number of items sold each month.

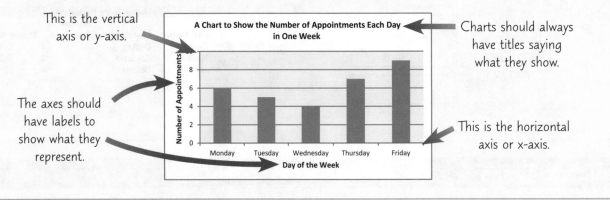

This is the vertical axis or y-axis.

Charts should always have titles saying what they show.

The axes should have labels to show what they represent.

This is the horizontal axis or x-axis.

Line Graphs `L1` `L2`

1) Line graphs are similar to bar charts, but a **line** is used to show the data.

2) They're used to plot **continuous data** — data that can have **any value** in a range.

3) For example, weight loss each month or temperature on different dates.

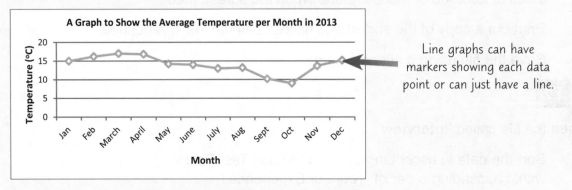

Line graphs can have markers showing each data point or can just have a line.

4) Line graphs are good for **comparing** two sets of data or for **larger** data sets.

Scattergraphs or X-Y Charts L1 L2

1) These are good for showing the **relationship** between **two** sets of **continuous data**.

2) Use these when **all the data** you need to plot is in **number** form.

3) For example, how temperature varies over time or how house prices change over the years.

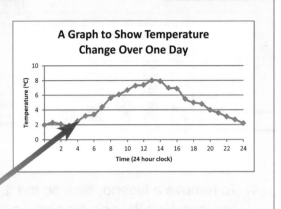

Scattergraphs can have just markers showing each data point or can have markers and a line.

Pie Charts L1 L2

1) They show the **relative sizes** of each piece of data.

2) They're used when you want to show what the **data total** is **made up of**.

3) For example, to show what a budget is spent on.

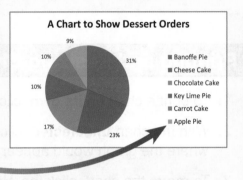

In a pie chart, you need a legend (key) to explain what each slice means (see p. 82).

All Charts Need a Title and Axis Labels L1 L2

1) You'll usually **add** and **edit** these **after** you've made your chart.

2) To **add a title**, click on your chart, then '**Layout**' in the '**Chart Tools**' tab.

3) Click the '**Chart Title**' button, and then choose **where** you want the title to go.

4) A text box for the title will appear — click in it to **edit** the **text**.

5) To add **axis labels** click '**Axis Titles**' on the '**Layout**' tab. Then choose the ones you want and **where** they should go.

6) A text box will appear — click in it to **edit** the **text**.

7) The axis titles are usually the **column titles** from the data in the spreadsheet.

8) Each should **describe** what that axis shows and should have **units** if required.

If you need to move titles or labels, click on them and drag.

9) **Titles** need to describe what the **whole chart** shows — be **specific**, especially if **years** or **dates** are involved, and make sure to use **capitals** where sensible but **not full stops**.

Section Six — Charts and Graphs

82

Legends `L1` `L2`

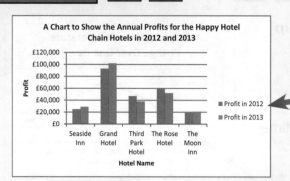

1) Sometimes you'll plot **more than one** set of data on a **single chart**.

2) The **legend** (key) shows how the **different sets** of data are represented.

3) If a chart has only **one set** of data, a legend **isn't needed**, so **remove** it.

4) To remove a legend, click on the '**Legend**' button on the '**Layout**' tab then click '**None**'. Or click on its box and press **delete**.

5) The legend **labels** come from **cells** in the **spreadsheet**. So to **edit** them, **change** the **text** in the correct cell.

Printing and Resizing Charts and Graphs `L1` `L2`

1) To print a chart on **its own**, click on the chart and then click '**Print**' in the '**File**' tab.

2) With the chart **unselected**, click '**Print**' in the '**File**' tab to see where the graph would appear if you printed the spreadsheet.

3) To **move** the chart, click the '**Home**' tab, then **click** on the chart and **drag** it to a new place.

4) To change the **area** of the **spreadsheet** being printed, look at page 82.

5) Use the '**Copy**' and '**Paste**' buttons to **add the chart** into a **new document** (like a word processing file).

6) To **change the size** of your chart, hover over one **corner** until a double-arrow symbol appears — a bit like this ⤢. Then **click and drag** to the size you want.

Practice Tasks

`L1` `L2`

1) Open the file called '**Farms**'.

 a) Add the title 'Grain Produced by Local Farms' to the chart.

 b) Add suitable axis labels.

 c) Save the file with a suitable name.

`L1` `L2`

2) Open the file called '**Theme_Park**'.

 a) Format the chart so it's clear and easy to read. (Hint: Think title, labels and legend.)

 b) Print out the chart and the spreadsheet data on one page.

Section Six — Charts and Graphs

Bar or Column Charts

How to Make a Column Chart L1 L2

1) A **bar** or **column chart** is a **simple** way of showing information.

2) Make sure you **understand what data** you need to plot **before** you start.

3) You might even need to **sort** your data before you plot it (see p 78).

Example 1

Create a **chart** showing the **profits** for the Happy Hotel chain hotels in **2012**.

	A	B	C
1	Hotel Name	Profit in 2012	Profit in 2013
2	Seaside Inn	£ 25,000	£ 29,000
3	Grand Hotel	£ 93,000	£ 102,000
4	Third Park Hotel	£ 47,000	£ 38,000
5	The Rose Hotel	£ 60,000	£ 52,000
6	The Moon Inn	£ 19,000	£ 21,000

1) **Select** the data you want to plot. Here you need the **names** of the hotels and the **2012 data**. Include the **column titles**.

2) Click the '**Insert**' tab and the '**Column**' button.

3) Click on the first option in '**2-D Columns**' called '**Clustered Column**'.

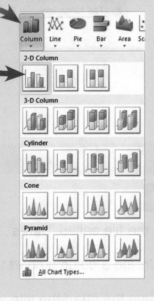

4) Format the chart so it has a **suitable title**, **labels** and the **legend** is **removed** (see p. 81-82).

Example 2

Create a **chart** showing the **profits** for the five Happy Hotel chain hotels in **2013**.

1) **Select** the data you want to plot.

2) This time it's **names** of the hotels and the **2013 data**. So select the **names first** then hold '**Ctrl**' and select the **2013 data** (plus column titles).

3) Click the '**Insert**' tab and follow the same instructions as in Example 1.

	A	B	C
1	Hotel Name	Profit in 2012	Profit in 2013
2	Seaside Inn	£ 25,000	£ 29,000
3	Grand Hotel	£ 93,000	£ 102,000
4	Third Park Hotel	£ 47,000	£ 38,000
5	The Rose Hotel	£ 60,000	£ 52,000
6	The Moon Inn	£ 19,000	£ 21,000

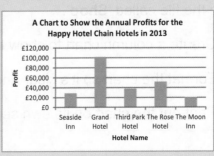

More Complicated Column Charts `L1` `L2`

You might need to plot **more than one** data set on a **single chart**.

Example

Create a chart to show the profits for the five
Happy Hotel chain hotels in **2012 and 2013**.

1) Select the **names**, **2012** and **2013 data**. Include the **column titles**.

2) Click the '**Insert**' tab and follow the instructions from Example 1 on page 83.

3) **Don't remove** the **legend** this time though — you need one
   when you have **more than one** data set on a chart.

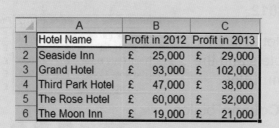

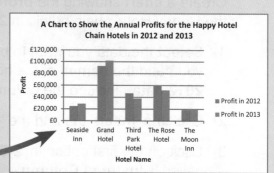

This type of chart is good for comparing two sets of data.

Practice Tasks

`L1` `L2`

1) Open the file called '**Sales**'.

   a) Create a column chart to show the sales figures for each member of the team in May.

   b) Give the chart the title 'A Chart to Show the Sales Figures for the Team in May',
      the y-axis label 'Number of Sales' and the x-axis label 'Sales Team Member'.

   c) Remove the legend.

   d) Insert the chart into a word processing document.

   e) Save the word processing file using a suitable name.

`L1` `L2`

2) Open the file called '**Shop**'.

   a) Create a column chart to show the total amount of money made from each item.

   b) Format the chart so it's clear and easy to read.

   c) Print out the chart on its own separate sheet.

Line Graphs and Scattergraphs

How to Make a Line Graph L1 L2

Line graphs are made in a **similar way** to column charts — select the data, click on your chart option then format it so it has good titles, labels and a legend if needed.

Example 1

Create a chart showing the **sales** at the **Bristo Square** coffee stall from **January to July**.

1) **Select** the data you want to plot. Include the **column titles**.

2) Click the 'Insert' tab and the 'Line' button.

3) Click on the first option in '**2-D Line**' called '**Line**'.

4) Format the chart so that it has a **suitable title**, **labels** and the **legend** is **removed** (see p. 81-82).

	A	B	C	D
1	Month	Bristo Square	Causewayside	Grindlay Street
2	January	£2,500	£2,000	£2,350
3	February	£2,250	£1,970	£2,200
4	March	£2,100	£2,100	£2,000
5	April	£2,060	£1,800	£1,950
6	May	£1,990	£1,750	£1,900
7	June	£1,700	£1,500	£1,800
8	July	£1,600	£1,200	£1,500

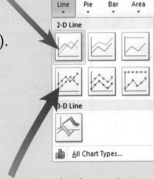

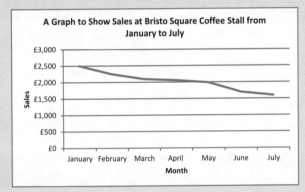

If you want the data points to have markers, choose the 'Line with Markers' option.

Example 2

Create a chart showing the sales at the **Bristo Square** and **Grindlay Street** coffee stalls from **January to July**.

1) **Select** the data you want to plot.

2) This time it's the **months**, the **Bristo Square** data and the **Grindlay Street** data. So select the **months** and the **Bristo Square** data **first** then hold '**Ctrl**' and select the **Grindlay Street data**. Include the **column titles**.

3) Click the 'Insert' tab and follow the same instructions as in Example 1. **Don't remove** the legend this time though.

	A	B	C	D
1	Month	Bristo Square	Causewayside	Grindlay Street
2	January	£2,500	£2,000	£2,350
3	February	£2,250	£1,970	£2,200
4	March	£2,100	£2,100	£2,000
5	April	£2,060	£1,800	£1,950
6	May	£1,990	£1,750	£1,900
7	June	£1,700	£1,500	£1,800
8	July	£1,600	£1,200	£1,500

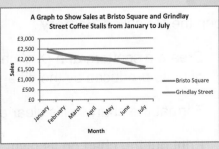

Scattergraphs or X-Y Charts `L1` `L2`

1) Scattergraphs are like a **special line graph**.

2) Use these when you need to plot **all number data**.

> **Example**
>
> Create a chart showing how the **height** of a child changes with **age**.
>
> 1) **Select** the data you want to plot. Include the **column titles**.
>
> 2) Click the 'Insert' tab and the 'Scatter' button.
>
> 3) You can choose 'Scatter with only Markers' or 'Scatter with Smooth Lines and Markers'.
>
> 4) Format the chart so that it has a **suitable title**, **labels** and the **legend** is **removed** (see p.81-82).

	A	B
1	Age of Child (years)	Height of Child (cm)
2	2	85
3	3	96
4	4	102
5	5	108
6	6	115
7	7	121
8	8	125
9	9	130
10	10	136
11	11	143
12	12	146
13	13	155
14	14	161
15	15	170
16	16	172
17	17	175
18	18	177

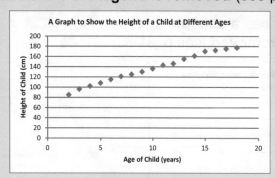

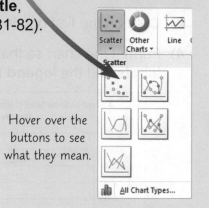

Hover over the buttons to see what they mean.

Practice Tasks

`L1` `L2`

1) Open the file called '**Wash**'.

   a) Create a line graph to show the sales for Washo-tron 3000 and Das Wash for all months.

   b) Give the graph the title 'A Graph to Show the Sales Performance of Dishwashers in 2013' and add x-axis and y-axis labels.

   c) Insert the graph into a word processing document.

   d) Save the word processing file using a suitable name.

`L1` `L2`

2) Open the file called '**Factory**'.

   a) Create a scattergraph (X-Y chart) to show the number of units produced by the different number of employees.

   b) Format the chart so it's clear and easy to read.

   c) Print out the chart on its own.

Pie Charts

How to Make a Pie Chart `L1` `L2`

Pie charts are quite **different** to column and
line charts but they're still **made** in a very **similar way**.

Example 1

Create a chart showing the **different costs** for a business.

1) **Select** the data you want to plot.
   Include the **column titles**.

2) Click the '**Insert**' tab and the '**Pie**' button.

3) Click on the first option in
   '**2-D Pie**' called '**Pie**'.

4) Format the chart so it has a suitable **title**,
   labels and **legend** (see next page).

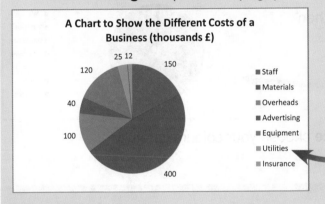

Make sure all the categories are shown
in the legend. If not, click and drag the
bottom edge of the graph to make it bigger.

Example 2

Create a chart showing the different costs for a business as **percentages**.

1) **Select** the data you want to plot. Include the **column titles**.

2) This time it's the **category** and the **percentage** of the total. So select
   the category first then hold '**Ctrl**' and select the percentage data.

3) Click the '**Insert**' tab and follow the same instructions as in Example 1.

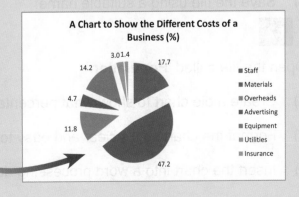

Choose 'Exploded Pie' (the 2nd
choice from the 'Pie' menu) to get
a chart which looks like this.

Data Labels Make Pie Charts Clearer `L1` `L2`

1) Titles and labels can be **added** and **edited** as on page 81.

2) You might need to **move** the **title** though so it doesn't **block** the chart.

3) You might also want to add **data labels**.

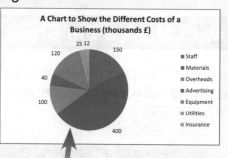

A Chart to Show the Different Costs of a Business (thousands £)

4) These will show the actual data for each **slice**. Add them by clicking the '**Data Labels**' button on the '**Layout**' tab in '**Chart Tools**'.

5) Click to choose where you want them to go. For example, '**Outside End**' like this chart.

Pie Chart Legends and Colours `L1` `L2`

1) A legend is **needed** in a pie chart to show what the **different slices** mean.

2) You can **change the colours** of the slices to make the chart **clearer**.

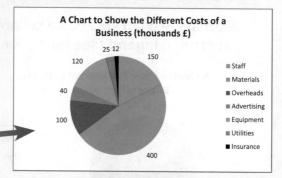

A Chart to Show the Different Costs of a Business (thousands £)

3) To do this, **click** on the **pie itself**, then **click again** to select one **slice**.

4) Then use the '**Fill Color**' button (looks like a paint bucket) on the '**Home**' tab to choose a colour.

5) If you're printing in **black and white** choose your colours carefully.

Practice Tasks

`L1` `L2`

1) Open the file called '**Electronics**'.

   a) Create a pie chart to show what proportion each of the products sold is of the total number of products sold.

   b) Give the chart a title and add 'Inside End' data labels to the chart.

   c) Save the file using a suitable name.

`L1` `L2`

2) Open the file called '**Population**'.

   a) Create a pie chart to show what percentage of the population live in each area.

   b) Format the chart so it's clear and easy to read.

   c) Insert the chart into a word processing document.

   d) Save the word processing document file using a suitable name.

Understanding Presentations

How to Use Presentation Software `EL3` `L1` `L2`

1) Presentation software is used when you **give talks**.

2) For example, you could use it when giving a talk on the **sales forecast** for a company.

3) Presentation software lets you create **slides**. A slide is like a page you can add text, images, videos, sound and animations to. You can use as many slides as you need.

4) During a presentation you move through the slides, showing them one at a time. This is called a **slide show**.

5) Here's an example of some slides created in **Microsoft® PowerPoint®**:

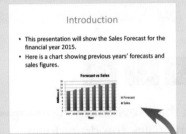

Presentations usually begin with a title slide. This lets the audience know what the presentation is about.

Adding charts or other images can help the audience follow what's being said and make the presentation more interesting.

Why Presentation Software is Useful `EL3` `L1` `L2`

1) Presentation software lets you **show** the audience information. This can make a talk easier to understand.

2) You can use the slides to make the **key points** stand out to the audience.

3) The slides can help you **remember** all the things you were planning to say in the talk.

Practice Task

`EL3` `L1` `L2`

1) a) Name two things you can add to a slide in presentation software.

    ....

   b) Give one reason that presentation software is useful when giving a talk.

    ....

Making Presentations — The Basics

What PowerPoint® Looks Like `EL3` `L1` `L2`

The presentation software used in this section is called Microsoft® PowerPoint®. Here's what you'll see when you open up a PowerPoint® document:

The slide pane will show you a list of all the slides in your presentation and let you move between them.

The slide selected in the slide pane will be shown here, in the slide area. You can add text and images to the slide.

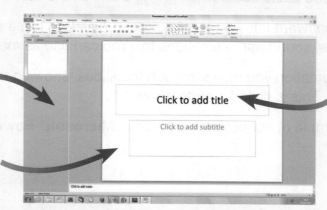

When you first open a presentation document, the title slide may be the only one there.

Adding Slides `EL3` `L1` `L2`

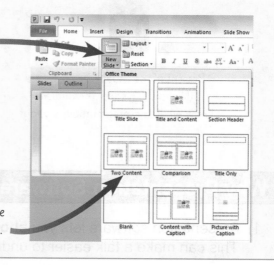

1) To add a new slide click the '**New Slide**' button on the 'Home' tab. Click the drop down menu to choose from different **slide layouts**.

2) The new slide will appear **after** the one that's shown on the **slide area**.

3) You can **delete slides** by right clicking on them in the slide pane and clicking '**Delete Slide**'.

The names of the different slide layouts are shown underneath.

Adding Text to Slides `EL3` `L1` `L2`

1) When a new slide is created, it will usually have **text boxes** on it.

2) For example, this one has two — one is for the slide's **title**, the other is for the **main text**.

3) If you want to add another text box, click on the 'Insert' tab and choose '**Text Box**'. Then draw the text box on the slide.

4) Either type straight into the text boxes or paste text in from another document.

5) You can resize text boxes by clicking on them and dragging the boxes that appear on their edges. You can also move them to different places on the slide.

Adding Images to Slides   EL3   L1   L2

1) You can add **images** and **shapes** to your presentation.

2) Click on the slide you want to add the image to, then click on the '**Insert**' tab.

To add an image that's saved on your computer, click on 'Picture', find the file you want to add, then click 'Insert'.

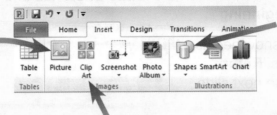

You can draw shapes on the slides. For example, arrows, stars and flowchart symbols.

To find a clip art image, click on 'clip art', type what you'd like a picture of into the search bar and click 'Go'. Click on the picture you want to add from the results.

3) You can also **copy** images from other documents and **paste** them onto a slide.

4) You may want to **resize** graphics by clicking on them and dragging the corners.

Moving Slides Around   EL3   L1   L2

1) You can **move slides** to different positions in the presentation.

2) In the slides pane, left click on the slide you want to move and **drag** it to a **new position**.

Adding Footers   EL3   L1   L2

1) A footer is a box which appears at the **bottom** of a slide. You can put your own text, the slide number, or the date in the footer.

2) Click on the '**Header & Footer**' button on the 'Insert' tab and this box will appear:

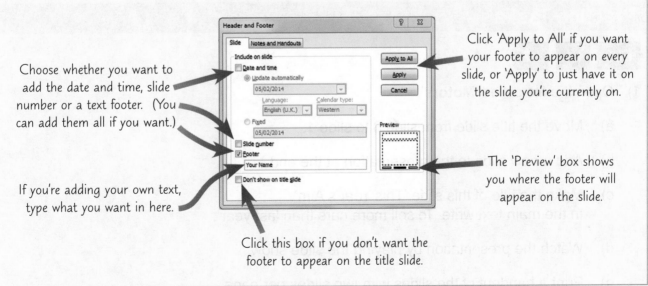

Choose whether you want to add the date and time, slide number or a text footer. (You can add them all if you want.)

Click 'Apply to All' if you want your footer to appear on every slide, or 'Apply' to just have it on the slide you're currently on.

If you're adding your own text, type what you want in here.

The 'Preview' box shows you where the footer will appear on the slide.

Click this box if you don't want the footer to appear on the title slide.

Playing Slide Shows EL3 L1 L2

1) When you're giving a presentation, the **slide show** option shows your slides, in the right order, on the full screen.

2) To begin a slide show, click on the '**Slide Show**' tab and select '**From Beginning**'.

3) When the slide show begins, left click or press '**Return**' to move on to the next slide.

To begin the slide show from the slide you're on, click the 'From Current Slide' button.

4) During a slide show, there are small **forward** and **back** arrows on the bottom left-hand side of the slides. You can click on these to move forward or back a slide.

Saving and Printing Slides EL3 L1 L2

1) Use '**Save**' and '**Save As**' on the '**File**' tab to save presentations.

2) You may want to **print out** your slides and give them to the audience as **handouts**.

3) Click on the '**File**' tab and select '**Print**'.

4) You can choose to print **all** the slides or just **some**.

5) There are different options for how you want the handouts to look here.

6) To print **two slides** on each page, select the '**2 Slides**' option from the drop-down menu.

Practice Tasks

EL3 L1 L2

1) Open the file called '**Motors**'.

   a) Move the title slide from slide 3 to slide 1.

   b) Add a new slide to the presentation at the end.

   c) Make the title of this slide 'This Year's Aim'. In the main text write 'To sell more cars than last year'.

   d) Watch the presentation by playing the slide show.

   e) Print a handout of the slides with two slides per page.

EL3 **L1** **L2**

2) Open the file called '**Holiday**'.

a) Insert a new slide after slide 3 with a 'Two Content' layout.

b) Open the file '**Holiday_Content**'. Copy the title from '**Holiday_Content**' and paste it into the new slide.

c) Copy 'Text 1' from '**Holiday_Content**' and paste it into the left-hand text box in the new slide.

d) Copy 'Text 2' from '**Holiday_Content**' and paste it into the right-hand text box in the new slide.

e) Copy the two images from '**Holiday_Content**' and paste them onto the slides. Place them below the correct text.

f) Add a text footer which says 'CGP Holidays' to every slide in the presentation apart from the title slide.

EL3 **L1** **L2**

3) Open a new, blank presentation document.
You're going to make a presentation about yourself.

a) Set up the presentation so that it has four slides.

- The title slide should have your name on it and an image.

- Slide 2 should have four pieces of information about you on it. For example, your date of birth, where you live, your job, any qualifications you have.

- Slide 3 should have some information about the town or city you live in.

- Slide 4 should say what your interests are.

b) Add a footer to every slide with your name on it.

c) Make sure each slide has an appropriate heading.

d) Play the slide show through.

e) Print a handout of the presentation with two slides per page.

Editing Slides

Editing Text   EL3   L1   L2

1) It's useful to use text of different **size**, **font** and **colour** in presentations. It can help highlight a point and make the slides more attractive.

2) Use the options in the '**Font**' and '**Paragraph**' sections of the '**Home**' tab to format text.

Click and choose from the list to change the font (style of the text).

Click here to change the size of the text.

Use these buttons to change how the text is aligned.

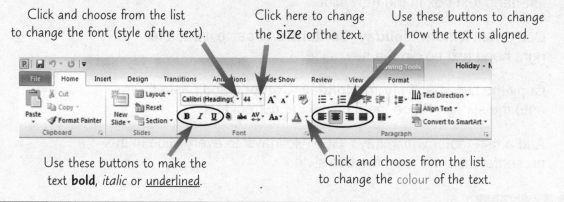

*Use these buttons to make the text **bold**, italic or underlined.*

Click and choose from the list to change the colour of the text.

Bullet Points and Numbered Lists   EL3   L1   L2

1) In presentations, it's a good idea to break up text into smaller chunks by using **bullet points** or **numbered lists**.

2) Just highlight the text, then click the '**Bullets**' or '**Numbering**' buttons on the '**Home**' tab.

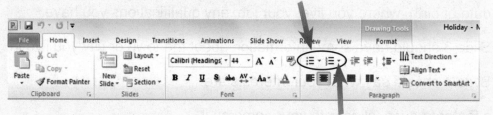

Use the drop-down menus to see different options.

3) Remove the bullets or numbers by highlighting the text and clicking the buttons again.

Changing the Background Colour of Slides   EL3   L1   L2

1) You can make a presentation more colourful by changing the background of slides.

2) Click on '**Background Styles**' in the '**Design**' tab then select '**Format Background**'. You'll see this box:

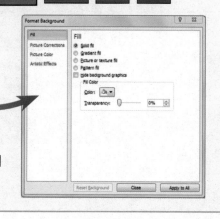

3) Choose a **fill style** and a **background colour**.

4) Clicking '**Close**' will add the background to the selected slide. '**Apply to All**' adds the background to all slides.

Practice Tasks

EL3 **L1** **L2**

1) Open the file called '**Olympics**'.

   a) Format the main text on slide 2 so that it's in bullet points.

   b) Change the font size of the main text to 24 pt.

   c) Change the background colour of all the slides to light blue.

   d) Save the file using a suitable name.

EL3 **L1** **L2**

2) Open the file called '**Pyramids**'.

   a) Change the font of the titles on both slides to 'Verdana'.

   b) Underline the titles on both slides.

   c) Change the font of the main text on slide 2 to 'Calibri'.

   d) Change the background colour of all the slides to light brown.

   e) Bold these words on slide 2 — 'Pharaohs', '100 000 workers', 'Giza' and 'The Pyramid of Khufu'.

   f) Save the file using a suitable name.

EL3 **L1** **L2**

3) Open the file '**Technology**'.

   a) Format the main text on slides 2 and 3 so that they're in numbered lists.

   b) Change the font size of the titles in slides 2 and 3 to 36 pt.

   c) Change the font size of the main text on slides 2 and 3 to 22 pt.

   d) Change the background colour of all the slides to light yellow.

   e) Make all the text on slide 1 dark blue. Make the titles on slides 2 and 3 dark blue.

   f) Bold the words before the hyphens in slides 2 and 3.
   For example, 'Television', 'Computers', 'Antibiotics'.

   g) Save the file using a suitable name.

More Editing Options

Adding a Table L1 L2

1) Click the 'Insert' tab and then the 'Table' button.

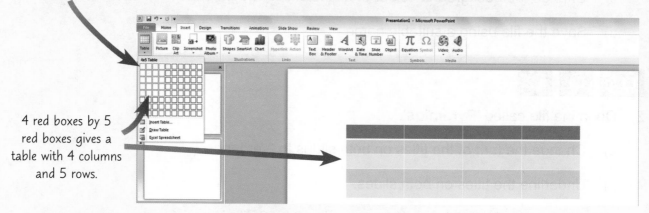

2) Choose the **size** of your table by moving your mouse over the boxes to **highlight** them and clicking when the right number of boxes are red.

4 red boxes by 5 red boxes gives a table with 4 columns and 5 rows.

3) To add **text** to a table, just click in a box and start typing.

4) You can use the '**Design**' and '**Layout**' tabs to make **changes** to a table. For example, you could change the colour or the border of a table, or change how the text is lined up.

Using Videos and Sound L1 L2

1) You can add a **video clip** or a piece of **audio** (sound) to your slides.

2) Click on either the '**Video**' or '**Audio**' button from the '**Insert**' tab.

3) Choose the option '**Video from File**' or '**Audio from File**'.

4) Then select the video or audio clip saved on your computer that you want to add.

Slide Transitions L2

1) **Transitions** are effects that change how each new slide **appears** in a slide show.

2) For example, a new slide could **swipe in** from the left, or you could have a '**page turning**' effect.

3) Choose a transition for a slide by clicking on it in the slide pane, then clicking on the '**Transitions**' tab and choosing from the options there.

Use 'Preview' to see how the transitions you've selected look.

Click 'None' to remove transitions.

4) You can choose a **different** transition for each slide or have the **same one** for each by clicking the '**Apply To All**' button.

Animations L2

1) You can add **animations** to **text** and **graphics**.

2) For example, you could make an image **appear from the left** or a text box **spin onto** the screen.

3) Select the object you want to add an animation to, then click on the '**Animations**' tab. Choose an animation from the options here.

Click 'Preview' to see how the animations you've selected look.

4) If you have more than one animated object on a slide, they'll appear in the **order** that the animations were **added** in. Numbered boxes beside each object **show** this order.

5) You can **change** the order of the animations or make them appear **all at once** using the '**Animation Pane**' on the 'Animations' tab.

6) To change the order of animations, **select** one and **drag** it to a new position.

7) To make all the animations appear at once, click the **drop down menu** beside each animation and select '**Start With Previous**'.

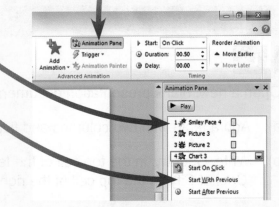

If you've not selected 'Start With Previous', you'll usually have to left click to start each animation when you're playing the slide show.

Creating Master Slides L2

1) A master slide is a **template**.

2) Each type of slide layout has **it's own** master slide. For example, there's a master slide for the 'Title and Content' layout and a different master slide for the 'Title Slide' layout.

3) **Changing** the master slide changes all of the slides with that layout in the presentation.

4) To change a master slide, click on the 'View' tab and select '**Slide Master**'.

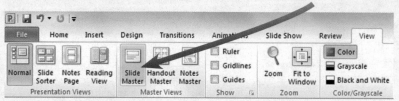

5) You are now in the '**Master View**'.

Select the master slide you want to change from the master slide pane. To see the names of different slide layouts, hover over the slide.

Make any changes to the master slide in the slide area. Edit the slide the same way as you would a normal slide.

When you've finished, click 'Close Master View'. The changes will automatically be applied to the slides that have the same layouts as the master slide you changed.

You can move text boxes around and change the font, size or colour of text.

You can also add images, which will appear on every slide with that layout.

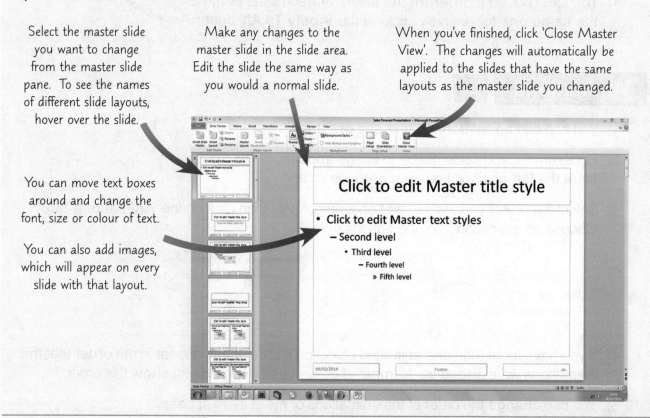

Practice Tasks

L1 L2

1) Open a new, blank presentation document. You only need one slide.

   a) Add a table with two columns and five rows to the presentation.

   b) Write 'Country' in the top cell of the left-hand column and 'Capital City' in the top cell of the right-hand column.

   c) Complete the table with the following information 'USA - Washington DC', 'UK - London', 'Japan - Tokyo', 'Sweden - Stockholm'. Save the file using a suitable name.

L2

2) Open the file called '**Rome**'.

    a)   Give each slide a different transition effect.

    b)   Give each graphic in the presentation a different animation effect.

    c)   Play the slide show through.

L2

3) Open the file called '**Safari**'.

    a)   Change the background colour of all the slides to green using the master slides.

    b)   Slide 2 has the layout type 'Title and Content'. Make these changes to its master slide:

        •   Change the heading font to 'Lucida Calligraphy'.

        •   Change the main text to 'Arial'.

        •   Copy the picture from the title page and paste it into the master slide.
Place it in the top right corner of the slide. Resize the image and
make the heading text box shorter to make room.

    c)   Slide 3 has the layout type 'Comparison'. Make the same
changes to its master slide as you made for slide 2.

    d)   Add the audio file '**Lion**' to the title page.

    e)   Play the slide show through.

> If your computer is not set
> up to play sound, you may
> not be able to do part d).

L2

4) Open the file called '**Circus**'.

    a)   Give each slide a transition effect.

    b)   Add an animation to the text on slide 2.

    c)   Give each graphic on slide 2 a different animation.

    d)   Order the animations so that the text appears first and the pictures appear in the order
they're written in the text.

    e)   Play the slide show through.

Advice for Presentations

Getting the Right Layout EL3 L1 L2

1) You should keep the **layout** of slides **simple**.

2) Make sure your slides are **consistent**.
This means the layout for all the slides should be **quite similar**.

3) Make sure you **divide** the presentation up **sensibly** onto the slides.
It's often a good idea to have one slide for each topic you want to talk about.

4) The layout should be **balanced**. Each slide should have a **similar amount** of material.

Text Layout EL3 L1 L2

1) Don't put too much text on your slides — the audience will find it difficult to read.

2) You want enough text to get your point across and no more. (You can always go into more detail when you're giving the presentation.)

3) **Bullet points** and **numbered lists** are a good way to cut down on text.

4) Use the same font and font size for the **main text** on each slide.

5) Most slides will have a **title**. Make sure it fits with what's on the slide.

6) Titles should have **larger** font size and possibly a **different** font than the main text.
Make sure all the titles have the same font and font size as each other.

7) Pick a font that is **easy to read** and make the font size **large** enough for people to see.

8) **Bolding**, *italicising* or <u>underlining</u> text can help make the important points
stand out but don't use them too much.

Images Layout EL3 L1 L2

1) Some images are there to **show information**, like charts or graphs.

2) Others are there to make the slides look more **interesting**.

3) Images should be **linked** to your presentation. For example, if a presentation is about London, a picture of Big Ben would be suitable. A picture of the White House wouldn't be.

4) When you're choosing images, think about what the **point** of each one is.

5) Think about the kind of images your audience will expect — some presentations are quite **serious**, in others you can use images that are a bit more fun.

6) Images should be **big enough** to be seen clearly but they shouldn't take over the slide.

7) Don't use **too many** images. It can be distracting for the audience.

Don't Overdo Animations and Transitions `L2`

1) A few animations can make a slide show more interesting.

2) Don't use too many though — having text and graphics whizzing all over the screen could be **distracting** to the audience.

3) For a **serious** presentation, it's better to pick **less flashy** slide transitions. For example, the '**Fade**' or '**Push**' options.

Check Your Presentation `EL3` `L1` `L2`

Always make sure you check your presentation before you finish.

1) Have a look at the layout of the slides and make sure no graphics **overlap** text.

2) Check the **spelling** and **grammar**. Use the **spellcheck** by clicking on the 'Review' tab and selecting '**Spelling**'.

Spelling

3) Always **run** the slide show before giving the presentation to make sure everything works as you want it to.

Practice Tasks

`EL3` `L1` `L2`

1) Open the file called '**Profit**'.

   a) Make the titles of slides 2 and 3 a suitable size.

   b) Check the layout of the slides and correct any errors.

   c) Find and correct any spelling mistakes.

`EL3` `L1` `L2`

2) Open the file called '**Coffee**'. Edit the format and layout of the slides so that they are suitable for a professional presentation. Think about the font types and sizes that are used and the layout of the slides. Check the spelling of the text and run the slide show through.

`EL3` `L1` `L2`

3) Make a presentation for a Recruitment Open Day at Huntersfield Nuclear Power Station.

   The presentation must have 4 slides, including a title slide. Make sure the layout is consistent, is clear and easy to read and has no mistakes.

   The presentation should include:

   • All the text from the file '**Recruitment_Text**'.

   • Some suitable images from the file '**Recruitment_Images**'.

   • Suitable formatting.

Database Basics

A Database Stores Data `L1` `L2`

1) A **database** is an organised collection of **data** (information), held in **records**.

2) Each record has data arranged into **fields** (categories), like names, addresses and phone numbers.

3) Records can hold different **types of data**, such as text, numbers, dates and currency.

4) So that no two records are exactly the same, they have a **unique identifier**. This is a field containing data that is different for each record, like an ID number.

Example

This is the unique identifier.

This is a record.

This is a field with the field name 'Job Title'.

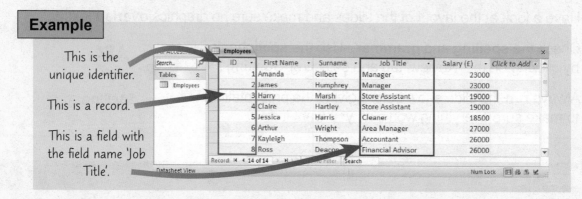

Databases and Spreadsheets are Similar `L1` `L2`

1) Databases are similar to spreadsheets, but they're better for certain tasks.

2) Databases have better tools for searching and displaying data.

3) You can search for data in databases using **queries**.

4) You can create **reports** from databases which show only the data you want to display.

> If you're asked for a 'report' or 'query', use a database, not a spreadsheet.

Setting up a Database `L1` `L2`

1) To create a database, use a program like Microsoft® Access®. We have used Access® throughout this section.

2) Click '**New**' from the 'File' tab. Select '**Blank database**', type a name, and click '**Create**'.

3) Once set up, all changes to data in the database will **save automatically**.

4) Data is stored in **tables**. Most programs will create a table for you when you create the database.

5) You can add more tables to the same database.

Setting Up Fields L1 L2

1) Before you enter any data, you need to set up some **fields** for your **table**.

2) This is done in '**Design View**'. Click this icon on the 'Home' tab.

3) One field needs to be the **unique identifier** or **primary key**.
Microsoft® Access® will create an ID field for you automatically,
but in other programs you may have to set one up yourself.

4) Type in titles for each of your fields in the '**Field Name**' column.

5) For each field choose a '**Data Type**' for the data that will go in the field.

6) For example, names should be '**Text**' and money should be '**Currency**'.

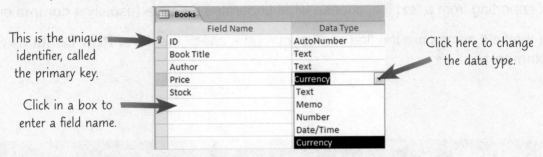

This is the unique identifier, called the primary key.

Click in a box to enter a field name.

Click here to change the data type.

7) You can set **rules** to limit what data goes in a field.
This is done to prevent mistakes when entering data.

8) For example, if a date should always be after 1/1/2000,
you could set a '**Validation Rule**' to only allow later dates in that field.

9) When you've set up your fields, click on the '**View**' button again to go back to the table.

Entering, Editing and Deleting Records L1 L2

1) In your table, each **row** is a different **record**, and each **column** is a different **field**.

2) To **enter** data, click in a box and start **typing**.

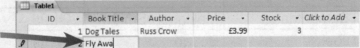

3) You can change the **width** of the field column. To do this, **hover** over the edge of the column heading, and **click** and **drag** when you see the ◄╫► icon.

4) To **edit** the data, just click in the box and make the change.

5) To **delete** a record, click on the bar to the left of it then press the '**Delete**' key.
Then click '**Yes**' to delete the selection.

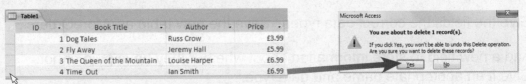

Be careful when deleting records. It can't be undone.

Importing Data into a Table 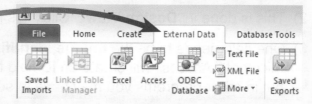 L1 L2

1) You can put data from another document into your database.

2) To do this, use the '**External Data**' tab.

3) Choose the type of document the data is stored in, such as a '**Text File**' or an '**Excel® spreadsheet**'.

4) You'll then be asked to browse for the file. Select it, then click '**Open**'.

5) You can create a new table for the data, or add it to a table you've already made. When you've chosen, click 'OK', then follow the instructions.

6) If importing from a text file, choose what separates the data (usually a **comma** or **tab**).

7) If the field names are the first row in your data, check the '**First Row Contains Field Names**' box.

Practice Tasks

L1 **L2**

1) Create a new database. Save your database and table as '**Orders**'.

    a) Add the following field names to your table, together with the correct data types: ID, First Name, Surname, Amount Due, Order Date.

    b) Add the following records to your table. Make sure the field columns are wide enough to display all the information.

First Name	Surname	Amount Due	Order Date
John	Wilkins	£15.50	26/02/2014
Nigel	Walker	£14.97	12/03/2014
Samantha	Makinson-Smith	£24.95	25/03/2014
Joel	Bough	£17.99	02/04/2014

    c) Mr. Wilkins has called to cancel his order. Delete his record.

L1 **L2**

2) Import the records from the text file called '**MoreOrders**' into a new table.

    a) Give the fields the correct data types. Save the new table as 'MoreOrders'.

    b) Add a new field to store information about whether they have paid or not. Give it an appropriate name and data type.

    c) Only Sam Jackson and Dawn Jones have paid so far. Enter this data into the new field.

Sorting and Filtering Data

Sorting Puts Records in Order   L1   L2

1) Sorting can make it much easier to find the records that you want, by rearranging them into a particular order.

2) A common way to sort **names** is alphabetically.
   This can be done two ways — '**Ascending**' (A-Z) and '**Descending**' (Z-A).

3) **Numbers** can also be sorted in two ways —
   'Ascending' (small to large), and 'Descending' (large to small).

4) Sorting **dates** in ascending order puts the records from oldest to newest, and descending order gives you the reverse.

Example

1) You want to sort a table of employees' information **alphabetically by surname**.

2) Click on the **field name** you want to sort the records with. In this case it's 'Surname'.

3) From the 'Home' tab, click '**Ascending**'.

Click to undo the sorting.

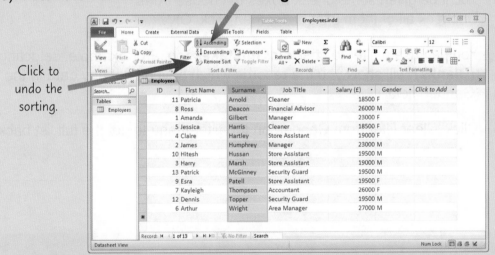

4) To sort in a different way, click '**Remove Sort**', then choose a new field and select 'Ascending' or 'Descending'.

5) You might want to sort the employees by **salary**, **largest to smallest**.

6) Select the 'Salary' field, then click '**Descending**'.

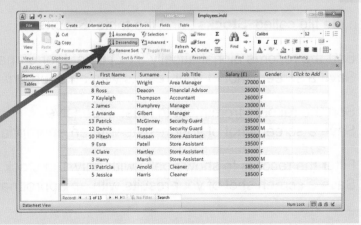

Filtering Just Displays Certain Records L1 L2

Filtering allows you to find records that contain certain bits of data.

Example

1) You want to filter the employees' information to just display the female employees.

2) Click on the 'Gender' field name, and select '**Filter**' on the 'Home' tab.

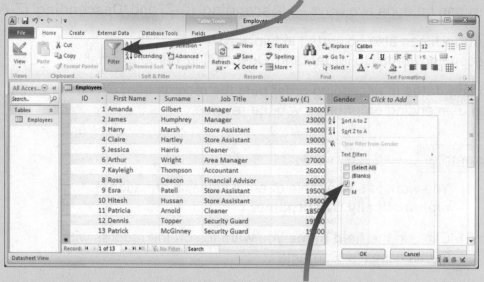

3) You'll be given some check boxes to choose from.
   Uncheck all of them except 'F', then click 'OK'.

4) You can use a filter to check for **mistakes** too. For example, selecting '**(Blanks)**' will show you the records which haven't got any data in the 'Gender' field.

5) Click 'Clear filter from Gender' on the filter menu to get the full list back.

Practice Task

 L1 L2

1) Open the file called '**Stocks**', and the table '**Stocks**'.

   a) Sort the records alphabetically (A-Z) by author surname.
      Save a screen shot of your results with an appropriate file name.

   b) Sort the records from most to least expensive.
      Save a screen shot of your results with an appropriate file name.

   c) Filter the records to show books with only 1 in stock.
      Save a screen shot of your results with an appropriate file name.

Queries and Reports

Create a Query to Search Records `L1` `L2`

Queries find records that fit certain **criteria** (rules).

Example

You want to use a query to show male employees in alphabetical order.

1) On the '**Create**' tab, click '**Query Design**':

2) Select the table you want to use.
   Your screen will look like this:

The Employees table has been selected for the query.

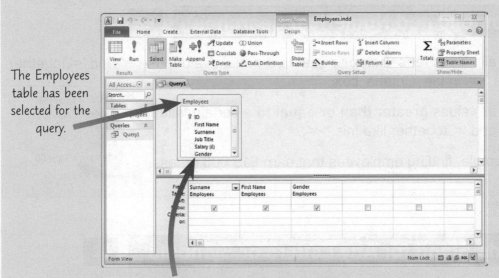

3) Double-click the fields you want to **sort**, **filter** or **display**.
   Here you need 'Surname', 'First Name' and 'Gender'.

4) All the men in the database have an 'M'
   in the 'Gender' field, so type **"M"** into
   the 'Criteria' box under 'Gender':

Field:	Surname	First Name	Gender
Table:	Employees	Employees	Employees
Sort:			
Show:	✓	✓	✓
Criteria:			"M"
or:			

> When searching for a word or letter, type it inside **double quotes**.

5) You only need to show the names. Uncheck the '**Show**' box in 'Gender'.

Field:	Surname	First Name	Gender
Table:	Employees	Employees	Employees
Sort:	Ascending		
Show:	✓	✓	
Criteria:			"M"
or:			

6) To sort the men into alphabetical order, click on the '**Sort**' box under 'Surname', then select '**Ascending**'.

7) Press the '**Run**' button on the 'Query Tools' tab to bring up the results in a new table.

8) To edit your query again, click the '**View**' button on the 'Home' tab.

Surname	First Name
Deacon	Ross
Humphrey	James
Hussan	Hitesh
Marsh	Harry
McGinney	Patrick
Topper	Dennis
Wright	Arthur

Searching Numerical Data L1 L2

1) To find all the records with data that is **equal** to a certain value, use '=' in the '**Criteria**' box.
For example, finding employees that earn exactly £19 500.

Field:	Salary (£)
Table:	Employees
Sort:	
Show:	✓
Criteria:	=19500

2) To find all values **less than** (but not equal to) a certain value, use the '**<**' sign.

3) To find all values **bigger than** (but not equal to) a certain value, use the '**>**' sign.

4) To find all values that are **not equal** to a certain value, use the '<' and '>' together like this '**<>**'.
For example, finding employees that don't earn exactly £23 000.

Field:	Salary (£)
Table:	Employees
Sort:	
Show:	✓
Criteria:	<>23000
or:	

More Complicated Numerical Searches L2

1) To find all values **less than or equal to** a certain value, use '<' and '=' together like this '**<=**' in the 'Criteria' box.

2) To find all values **greater than or equal to** a certain value, use '>' and '=' together like this '**>=**'.

3) For example, finding employees that earn £19 000 or less.

Field:	Salary (£)
Table:	Employees
Sort:	
Show:	✓
Criteria:	<=19000

Wildcards Stand for Any Letters or Symbols L2

1) When searching **text** data, you can use a **wildcard** to replace letters and symbols.

2) You can use '*****' to stand for **any number** of letters or symbols.
For example, if you searched for 'A*', you would get records containing words like 'A', 'arm', 'Arnold', and 'antelope'.

3) You can use '**?**' to stand for a **single** letter or symbol. For example, if you searched for 'b?t', you would get results like 'bit', 'bat', 'bet' and 'but'.

Example

A company wants to view all employees whose surname begins with H.

1) In the criteria for 'Surname', type "**H***".

The database program may add the word 'Like', as it recognises this kind of query.

Field:	Surname	First Name	Salary (£)
Table:	Employees	Employees	Employees
Sort:			
Show:	✓	✓	✓
Criteria:	Like "H*"		
or:			

2) Click '**Run**'. You'll get all of the results that begin with H, regardless of how many letters are in the name.

Surname ▾	First Name ▾	Salary (£) ▾
Humphrey	James	23000
Hartley	Claire	19000
Harris	Jessica	18500
Hussan	Hitesh	19500

'And', 'Not' and 'Or' are called Logical Operators `L2`

1) You can use special words like '**And**', '**Not**', '**Or**' and '**Between**' in the 'Criteria' box to make more complicated queries.

2) Typing 'Not "cheese"' would find all records which are **not** 'cheese'.

3) Typing 'Between 6 And 9' would find all records with numbers **between** 6 **and** 9 (including 6 and 9) in that field.

4) Typing '"M" Or "F"' in the 'Gender' criteria box would find all the males and females.

Reports let you Format your Query `L1` `L2`

1) Database tables and queries can't be formatted properly.

2) Instead you can create a **report**, which can be formatted.

Example

1) Select the table or query you want to format, and click the '**Report**' button on the '**Create**' tab.

2) This will automatically create a report for you to format:

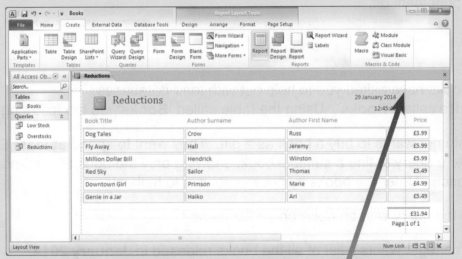

These broken lines show the printing area.
Resize the boxes so the data fits inside these lines or it won't print.

3) To **rearrange** boxes, click on them and drag them around.

4) To **sort** fields, **click** in the field then use the sort buttons in 'Home'.

5) To **resize** a box, click on it then hover over the edge until the ↔ symbol appears, then click and drag.

6) To **edit** the contents of a box, **click** on it then start **typing**. You can't edit the data from the query or table on the report screen.

7) Boxes can be **removed** by **selecting** them, then pressing '**Delete**'.

8) To change fonts and colours, use the '**Format**' tab.

9) The '**Page Setup**' tab allows you to change things like margins, orientation and paper size ready for printing.

Practice Tasks

L1 **L2**

1) Open the file called '**Laptops**'. Use the table called '**Laptops**' in the following tasks.

   a) A customer wants a laptop made by **Ultrawebb**. Create a query to find all of the Ultrawebb laptops, showing the processor, storage, RAM and price only.

   b) Save the query with an appropriate file name.

   c) A customer is looking for a laptop with **more than 700 GB** of storage. Create a query to find all the suitable laptops, showing the manufacturer, processor, storage, RAM and price.

   d) Save the query with an appropriate file name.

   e) A customer would like a laptop with an **i5 processor**. Create a query to find all the suitable laptops, listed in **price order** (lowest to highest). Show the manufacturer, storage, RAM and price only.

   f) Save the query with an appropriate file name.

   g) Create a report for each of the queries you made in parts a), c), and e), then print them off.

L2

2) TellTale Books have asked you to help out with their databases.
   Open the file called '**Books**'. Using the table called '**Books**', do the following:

   a) A customer wants to buy a book as a gift. They want to spend **at least £5.99**. Create a query to find a suitable book, showing only the book title, author name, and price. Order the books by price — lowest to highest.

   b) Save the query with an appropriate file name.

   c) The manager wants a list of all the books released in **January 2014**. Create a query to find these books, showing only the book title, author name, price and release date.

   d) Save the query with an appropriate file name.

   e) A customer is trying to buy a book for their daughter that was released **after January 2014**. They can't remember the author's first name, but think the surname **begins with P**. Create a query to find the book they want, showing only the book title and author name.

   f) Save the query with an appropriate file name.

   g) Create a report for each of the queries you made in parts a), c) and e), then print them off.

Test Help

Read the Paper Carefully

1) Read any **introduction notes** and the **questions** themselves carefully.

2) Make sure you understand:

   - what **information** you need to **write on the paper** (like your name),

   - what **files** you need to **use**, **where** they are and where they should be **saved**,

   - what you need to **print out** and what the printouts should have on them, and

   - any other **specific instructions** you need to follow.

3) **Read** the test quickly again at the **end** to **double-check** you've done everything.

Work Through Each Task and Question

1) The **test** is usually made up of a **number of tasks** based around one main **theme**. For example, you might be planning a party. This might involve using the internet, working on a spreadsheet and producing an invitation in a word processing program.

2) Each task will usually be broken down into **steps or questions**.

3) **Read** each task **carefully** before you start, then go through each step **one at a time**.

4) **Have a go at everything** — even just opening a file might help jog your memory.

5) If you **really can't** do one step, **move on** to the next one in that task. **Don't** just **skip ahead** to the next task — you might **miss out** on **easy marks**.

Timing and the Number of Marks

1) **Keep an eye** on the **time** — if you're **stuck** and time is moving on, **move on** to the next thing.

2) You can always **go back** to what you've missed if there's time at the **end**.

3) Usually, the **greater** the **number of marks**, the **more time** you need to spend on that task.

4) So don't spend **ages** on something that's only worth a **couple** of marks.

Choosing the Right Software Program

1) In the test you might have to **decide** what **program** to complete the tasks in.

2) There is some guidance to **help** you on page 10.

3) You should also **ask your tutor** as there might be particular programs your **exam board** won't allow you to use.

4) For example, you might be asked to make a **poster** using a program of your choice. A **word processing** or **presentation** program is suitable, but your exam board might not accept a file made with a presentation program.

Save Your Work as You Go

1) It's important to **keep saving** your work **regularly**.

2) This means you **won't lose anything** if something goes wrong or there's a power cut.

3) Look back at page 18 for more on **saving** and **naming files**.

4) Look carefully at **where** you're told to **save** files to — if the test doesn't say where, then choose somewhere **sensible** where your tutor will be able to **find them** easily.

Check Your Work Before Printing and Saving

1) Checking your work helps you to **spot mistakes** or parts of the test you've **missed**.

2) You should also check that your work looks **neat** and is **appropriate** for the task.

3) Check for **spelling errors** — these could lose you marks.
You can use a spellchecker in some programs (see p. 44 and p. 48).

4) Don't forget to **re-save** your document if you've made any changes.

Check Your Printouts

Make sure you check any printouts carefully before you hand them in.

- Do they contain all the **details needed**? For example, you might need to add your **name** to every printout otherwise they might not be marked.

- Can everything be **read clearly**? For example, make sure your search engine criteria (keywords) can be read. You might need to **resize** your work so it's larger.

- Does any **formatting** work? Does it look **neat and professional**? For example, if you've used a black and white printer, any **colours** chosen might not work.

Entry Level 3 Tasks

A friend has asked you to help her organise a charity raffle.

There are **three** tasks to complete. You will need to:

- work out the cost of the prizes,

- design a poster to advertise the raffle, and

- write an email to Susan about the raffle.

Task A — Work out the cost of the prizes

1.   Make sure you are sitting comfortably.

Start your computer system.

Open the file called '**Raffle_Prizes**'.

(3 marks)

2. (a)   The cost of the chocolates has increased.

Change the cost of the box of chocolates to £17.

(1 mark)

(b)   In cell B11, enter a formula to calculate the total cost of the prizes
in cells B4 to B10.

(1 mark)

3. (a)   Use formatting to make the name of the most expensive prize stand out.

(1 mark)

(b)   Use formatting to display the costs of the prizes as currency.

(2 marks)

4.   Save the spreadsheet.

(1 mark)

Total for Task A = 9 marks

Task B — Design a poster to advertise the raffle

1. (a)   Open the file called '**Raffle_Info**'.

(1 mark)

   (b)   Use the information given in '**Raffle_Info**' to make a poster advertising the raffle.

   Include the following in the poster:

   •   The cost of a raffle ticket.

   •   The date the raffle is being drawn.

   •   The prizes that can be won.

   •   Where raffle tickets are on sale.

(4 marks)

2.   Open the file named '**Logo_Password**'.

   Use the password in this file to open the file named '**Hospice_Logo**'.

   Insert the logo into a suitable place in the poster.

(4 marks)

3.   Use the Internet to find an photo of a garden bench.

   Insert the photo into the poster in a suitable place.

(3 marks)

4. (a)   Format the layout of the poster to make it look good.
   You could use the following:

   •   font sizes

   •   font styles

   •   bolding, underlining, italics and colour

   •   alignment

   •   bullet points

   •   page borders

(4 marks)

   (b)   Check the poster is suitable for purpose and contains no spelling errors.

(2 marks)

5.   Save the poster.

   Print the poster.

(2 marks)

Total for Task B = 20 marks

Task C — Send an email message

1.   Open the file called '**Email**'.

Read the email in the file.

(1 mark)

2.   Write a new email replying to Susan's email.

You worked out the total cost of raffle prizes in your spreadsheet.

Put the total cost of raffle prizes into the email.

Answer the other questions in your reply.

(7 marks)

3.   Check your reply for mistakes.

Print out your reply. (You do not need to send the email.)

(2 marks)

4.   Shut down your computer system correctly.

(1 mark)

Total for Task C = 11 marks

End of Entry Level 3 Tasks

Level 1 Tasks

You are going to help a colleague organise a Christmas Party.

You'll need to access the following files:

- **Evidence_Doc_L1**
- **Party_Graphics**
- **Party_Costs**
- **CGP_Logo**
- **Food_Suppliers**
- **Food_Details**
- **Party_Details**
- **Transport**

At the end of the tasks make sure you have printed out all the evidence required, including your completed '**Evidence_Doc_L1**' file.

Make sure your name is clearly written or printed on every printout produced.

Part A — You can use the internet for this part only.

Task 1 — Eccle Riggs Hall

The party is going to be held at CGP's head office — Eccle Riggs Hall.

Use the internet to find the full postal address for Eccle Riggs Hall.

Open the file '**Evidence_Doc_L1**' and enter the date and your name.

Put the following evidence into '**Evidence_Doc_L1**':

- A screen shot showing your search and results.
- The postal address of Eccle Riggs Hall.
- The URL where you found the address.

Save the changes you've made to '**Evidence_Doc_L1**'.

(4 marks)

Evidence

The correct evidence from your internet research pasted into the file '**Evidence_Doc_L1**' — screen shot, address and URL.

Total for Task 1 = 4 marks

Part B — You must not use the internet for this part.

Task 2 — Costs of the party

The party will cost some money.

(a)   Open the file '**Party_Costs**' to see a list of the costs linked to the party.

Enter a formula to calculate the total cost of the drinks and transport.

Enter a formula to calculate the total costs for the party.

(4 marks)

(b)   Make sure the spreadsheet is correctly formatted and is easy to read.

(3 marks)

(c)   Print out a copy of the spreadsheet showing the formulas that you've used.

(1 mark)

Evidence

A printout of your spreadsheet that shows the formulas used.

Total for Task 2 = 8 marks

Task 3 — Party food

Quotes for party food were collected from four different suppliers.

(a)   Open the file '**Food_Suppliers**' to see what each supplier quoted.

Create a chart to show the total quote from each supplier in ascending order of cost.

Make sure the chart is clearly labelled and easy to read.

Print out your chart on a separate sheet in landscape.

(9 marks)

(b)   Insert your chart into a new word processed document
and save the document as '**Task 3 chart**'.

Make the file '**Task 3 chart**' a read-only file.

Take a screen shot to show the file is read-only.

Insert the screen shot into '**Evidence_Doc_L1**' and save the document.

(3 marks)

Evidence

A landscape printout of your chart.

A screen shot showing '**Task 3 chart**' is read-only pasted into '**Evidence_Doc_L1**'.

Total for Task 3 = 12 marks

Task 4 — Poster to advertise the party

Create an A4 portrait poster to advertise the Christmas party to the staff.

(a)   The poster needs to include:

- Details of the party from the file '**Party_Details**'.

- The address of Eccle Riggs Hall (which you found in **Part A**, **Task 1**).

- Two appropriate graphics from the file '**Party_Graphics**'.

- The logo from the file '**CGP_Logo**'.

The poster must be clear, easy to read and contain no errors.

(13 marks)

(b)   Save the poster with a suitable name.

Print out your poster in A4 portrait orientation.

(2 marks)

> **Evidence**
>
> A printout of your completed poster in A4 portrait orientation.

Total for Task 4 = 15 marks

Task 5 — Presentation to senior managers

Create a presentation to show the different food options to the senior managers.

(a)   The presentation needs to include:

- A title slide with the title 'Christmas Party' and an image from '**Party_Graphics**'.

- The company logo from the file '**CGP_Logo**' on every slide.

- A slide with details about the food each supplier would provide from the file '**Food_Details**'.

- A slide containing the chart you made in **Part B**, **Task 3**.

The presentation must contain no errors and have a consistent format.

(12 marks)

(b)   Save the presentation with a suitable name.

Print a copy of the presentation slides with two slides on each page.

(2 marks)

> **Evidence**
>
> A printout of your completed presentation with two slides on each page.

Total for Task 5 = 14 marks

Task 6 — Transport arrangements

Transport to and from the party will be provided for staff who need it.

(a) Open the file '**Transport**' to see information about the transport for the party.

Matthew Scott no longer needs transport. Edit his record to show this.

Becky Potter can't go to the party. Delete her record from the table.

John Williams has just started working for CGP and needs transport from Broughton. Add his details to the table.

Take a screen shot of the table.

Insert the screen shot into '**Evidence_Doc_L1**' and save the document.

(4 marks)

(b) Create a query within '**Transport**' to find the records of the staff who need transport, sorted alphabetically by town name.

Show only the names of the staff and the town name.

Create and print a sorted report of the query on a single sheet of A4.

(4 marks)

Evidence

A screen shot of the edited table pasted into the file '**Evidence_Doc_L1**'.

A printout of the report on a sheet of A4.

Total for Task 6 = 8 marks

Task 7 — Email your poster

You need to send your poster file to the Production Department for printing.

Tom Woods is the Head of Production.

Write an email to Tom and ask him if the poster looks suitable.

Attach the poster file to the email.

Tom's email address is tom@cgpbooks.co.uk

Take a screen shot of the email you write. (You do not need to send the email.)

Insert the screen shot into '**Evidence_Doc_L1**' and save the document.

(6 marks)

Evidence

A screen shot of the prepared email pasted into the file '**Evidence_Doc_L1**'.

Total for Task 7 = 6 marks

Task 8 — Organise your work

You need to organise the files that you've created so they're easy to find.

Create some folders with suitable names and place your files into them.

Take a screen shot to show the folders you've created.

Insert the screen shot into the file 'Evidence_Doc_L1'.

(3 marks)

> **Evidence**
>
> A screen shot of the folders created pasted into the file 'Evidence_Doc_L1'.

Total for Task 8 = 3 marks

Task 9 — Questions

Write the answers to these questions on the dotted line underneath each question.

(a)   State **one** way that a file containing information about the costs of the Christmas party could be kept private.

....

....

(1 mark)

(b)   Which of the following is a website address (URL)?

chris@cgpbooks.co.uk

santa.jpeg

www.bbc.co.uk/news

cgpbooks.html

....

(1 mark)

Total for Task 9 = 2 marks

End of Level 1 Tasks

Level 2 Tasks

Wholesome Drinks is a Bristol based company that produce a range of healthy drinks. They are planning to attend a national food and drink trade show held in Birmingham. You are going to help organise their trip to the show.

You'll need to access the following files:

- **Evidence_Doc_L2**
- **Letter**
- **Costs_And_Orders**
- **Amanda_Harrop**
- **Logo**
- **Schedule_And_Aims**
- **Buyer_Data**
- **Buyer_Details**
- **Meetings**

At the end of the tasks make sure you have printed out all the evidence required, including your completed '**Evidence_Doc_L2**' file.

Make sure your name is clearly written or printed on every printout produced.

Part A — You can use the internet for this part only.

Task 1 — Travelling to the show

The food and drink show is going to be held at the NEC in Birmingham, UK.

Using the internet, find a train ticket website. Use the website to find the price for one person to travel tomorrow at any time from Bristol Temple Meads to Birmingham International, returning at any time on the next day.

Bookmark the web page where you found the ticket price.

Put the following evidence into the file '**Evidence_Doc_L2**':

- A screen shot(s) showing your search and results.

- The URL where you found the ticket price.

- A screen shot showing the bookmarked page.

(6 marks)

> **Evidence**
>
> The correct evidence from your internet research pasted into the file '**Evidence_Doc_L2**' — screen shots and URL.

Total for Task 1 = 6 marks

Task 2 — Email about train tickets

Write an email to Amanda Harrop with the details about the train tickets from Task 1.

Add Amanda to your email contacts list using the details from the file about her.

Let Amanda know that you've found the cost of the train.

Give the price for one person to travel to and from the show by train and the URL of the web page where you found it.

Take a screen shot of the email contacts list entry for Amanda.

Take a screen shot of the email you write. (You do not need to send the email.)

Insert the screen shots into the file 'Evidence_Doc_L2'.

(7 marks)

Evidence

A screen shot of the prepared contacts list entry and email for Amanda pasted into the file '**Evidence_Doc_L2**'.

Total for Task 2 = 7 marks

Part B — You must not use the internet for this part.

Task 3 — Meeting buyers at the show

Wholesome Drinks wants to invite some buyers to meet them at the show.
They only want to invite buyers who have ordered £25 000 or more in the last year.

(a)   You have been asked to edit a spreadsheet to calculate the total value of orders for the buyers in the last year. You have been given a file containing the data required.

Make sure the data is clear and formatted correctly.

(6 marks)

(b)   Use a function to automatically show 'Invite' if the total value of orders for last year is greater than or equal to £25 000. "Don't invite" should show next to all other buyers.

Print out your finished spreadsheet.

Print out a version showing the formulas used.

(8 marks)

Evidence

A data printout of the spreadsheet.

A formula printout of the spreadsheet.

Total for Task 3 = 14 marks

Task 4 — Invitation to buyers

You need to use mail merge to create letters for the buyers selected in Task 3, which will invite them to a meeting at the show.

You have been given a file with contact details for each buyer.
You also have a file that contains a template for the letter that you need to prepare.

Each letter must include the Wholesome Drinks logo and the date.

The letter must be easy to read and contain no errors.

Print out a copy of the unmerged letter showing the merge fields.

Print out copies of the merged letters to the 'Invite' buyers from Task 3 only.

(12 marks)

Evidence

A printout of the completed unmerged letter showing the merge fields.

Printouts of all of the merged letters sent out to the invited buyers only.

Total for Task 4 = 12 marks

Task 5 — Costs and benefits of attending the show

Wholesome Drinks have been to the food and drink show for the past 5 years.

Create a chart to show the cost of attending the show
and the value of orders taken at each of the shows.

You have been given a file that contains details of these cost and orders.

Make sure the chart is clearly labelled and easy to read.

Print out your chart on a separate sheet.

(7 marks)

Evidence
A printout of your completed chart on a separate sheet.

Total for Task 5 = 7 marks

Task 6 — Presentation for the sales team

Create a presentation about the show for your manager to present to the sales team.

(a) The presentation needs to include:

- A title slide containing the company logo and a suitable heading.

- A slide containing the schedule for the day that you have been given.

- A slide containing the aims for the day that you have been given. Add the total value of orders generated at the show in Year 5 (2013) to aim number 5.

- The chart you created in Task 5.

- The company name in a footer and the company logo in the top right of all slides (except the title slide).

- A slide transition.

The presentation must contain no errors and have a consistent format.

Take a screen shot to show the slide transition. Insert this into '**Evidence_Doc_L2**'.

Print handouts of your presentation with two slides on each page.

(18 marks)

(b) You need to organise the files used to create the presentation so they're easy for your manager to find.

Create a folder and place all the files you've used and created into it.

Take a screen shot to show the contents of the folder you've created.

Compress (zip) the folder and take a screen shot to show this.

Insert your screen shots into the file '**Evidence_Doc_L2**'.

(5 marks)

Evidence

A screen shot showing the slide transition pasted into '**Evidence_Doc_L2**'.

A printout of your handouts with two slides on each page.

A screen shot showing the contents of your folder pasted into '**Evidence_Doc_L2**'.

A screen shot showing the compressed folder pasted into '**Evidence_Doc_L2**'.

Total for Task 6 = 23 marks

Task 7 — Organising meetings

You need to organise meetings with buyers who have confirmed they will be there.

You have been given a file containing the names of these companies, contact names, and the date and time they're available to meet.

(a)   Import the data from the file into a new database table, making sure that each record has a unique identifier.

Take screen shots to show both the table and the data types assigned to each field. Insert the screen shots into '**Evidence_Doc_L2**'.

(5 marks)

(b)   Create a query to find the companies available for lunchtime or afternoon meetings on the 2nd of September 2014. Show the companies and meeting slots only.

Take a screen shot of your query criteria and insert it into '**Evidence_Doc_L2**'.

Create and print a report of the query on a single sheet of A4.

(6 marks)

Evidence

Screen shots pasted into the file '**Evidence_Doc_L2**' to show: the imported table, the data types and the query criteria.

A printout of the report on a sheet of A4.

Total for Task 7 = 11 marks

Task 8 — Questions

Write the answers to these questions on the dotted line underneath each question.

(a)   State **one** keyboard shortcut and describe what it is used for.

....

....

(2 marks)

(b)   Describe why you might put files into a compressed folder before attaching them to an email instead of attaching them all separately.

....

....

(1 mark)

Total for Task 8 = 3 marks

End of Level 2 Tasks

Answers — Practice Tasks

Section One — The Basics

Page 6

Q1 Successfully start up and shut down your computer using the information on page 4.

Q2 It's important to shut down a computer properly so that you don't lose or damage data.

Q3 Print screen or 'PrtScn'.

Q4 E.g.
Input devices: keyboard / mouse / scanner / digital camera microphone.
Output devices: printer / monitor / speakers / projector.
Both input and output devices: a touchscreen / a headset.

Page 8

Q1 Enaj2675Boo
This is good because it contains a mixture of letters and numbers, and it doesn't contain anything that's easy to guess.

Q2 Tangerine

Q3 Any one of, e.g: use and run up-to-date antivirus software / regularly scan your computer for viruses / don't open any files/ email attachments/ or download anything that might not be safe.

Page 10

Q1 Spreadsheet software.

Q2 Producing slide shows or handouts for a talk.

Q3 E.g. word processor.
As the document contains text and graphics word processor is suitable, but desktop publishing software or presentation software could be used.

Page 13

Q1 13.5

Q2 The red and white 'X' button.

Q3 Jellyfish, Koala and Penguins.
The pictures on your computer might not be the same as these — it'll depend on which operating system you have.

Page 16

Q1 Please see the file called Section_One.

Q2 Please see the file called Office_Task_Answer.
A sensible name is one that describes what is in the document. For example it might be 'Office Task Answer' or 'Recycle bin icon'.

Page 17

Q1 Click the 'Safely Remove Hardware and Eject Media' icon, then click 'Eject' for the device you want to remove.

Page 20

Q1 You should have a document with a sensible name saved in a folder called 'Reading'.
An example of a sensible name for this document is 'Favourite authors'.

Q2 Please see the file called Bread_Answers.

Page 21

Q1 a) E.g. increase the size of text / increase the size of icons / change the contrast settings.
Any sensible answer as long as it makes things easier to see.

b) E.g. reduce the speed at which you need to double-click.
Any sensible answer as long as it makes the mouse easier to use.

Page 22

Q1 b) E.g. make sure there's plenty of light where you are working / make sure there is no glare on the screen / change the monitor's contrast and brightness settings.

Page 24

Q1 Please see the file called Evidence_Answers.
The document should have been printed in landscape and saved with a sensible name.

Section Two — The Internet

Page 27

Q1 E.g. car insurance comparison.
You need to include comparison or a similar word. Only using car insurance will give you companies who sell insurance but not comparison websites.

Q2 a) Kew, Richmond, Surrey TW9 4DU
You should have carried out a search with keywords like 'National Archives Address'.

b) 01299 402114
You should have carried out a search with keywords like 'West Midlands Safari Park phone number'

Q3 E.g. When on the website, click the 'favourites' or 'bookmark' button on the browser tool bar. He might also need to click 'Add to favourites' too.

Page 29

Q1 a) Any suitable picture of the mountain with a suitable file name, e.g. OldMan.jpg.
You should have used keywords like 'Old Man of Coniston'. Then clicked on the images button on the results page.

b) Any suitable print out of a screen shot of a search engine results page showing keywords (search criteria) and a map of Lake Windermere. Please see the file called Windermere_Answer.
You should have carried out a search with keywords like 'Lake Windermere map'. Or 'Lake Windermere' and clicked on the maps button on the results page. Make sure you can see the keywords on your screen shot.

c) 9:30 am till 5:00 pm, 7 days a week.
You should have carried out a search using keywords like 'pencil museum Keswick'. Then found a page on the website showing the opening times.

Q2 Please see the file called
Vauxhall_Answer.
*Using the OR function means
websites with either or both 'Astra'
and 'Corsa' will be in the results.
Make sure you can see the
keywords on your screen shot.*

Page 32
Q1 Only the box next to 'Your
secure banking website'
should be ticked.
Q2 E.g. The UK government
website would be more reliable
because it is likely to be an
official site with up to date
information that you can trust.
Q3 Picture C. It's in the public
domain. The other two have
a watermark and a copyright
notice so you would have
to ask for permission.

Section Three — Email

Page 36
*Your answers might look different to the
ones we provide if you are using different
email software.*
Q1 Please see the file called
Jane_Email_Answer.
Q2 Please see the file called
IT_Email_Answer.
Q3 Please see the file called
Susan_Email_Answer.
*Make sure your email has the wet paint
sign file attached to it.*

Page 40
Q1 Please see the file called
Plumber_Email_Answer.
Q2 Please see the file called
Staff_Email_Answer.
*In this email you need to have used
three different email addresses: one that
the email is addressed to, one that the
email is Cc'd to and one that the email
is Bcc'd to.*
Q3 Please see the file called
Contact_Details_Answer.
*Your screen shots might look very
different if you're not using Outlook®
email software but you should still have
the same information shown.*
Q4 Please see the file called
Joshua_Temple_Answer.

Page 42
Q1 A screen shot showing a search
of your inbox for 'functional skills'.
Q2 a) The emails in your inbox
should be grouped by who
they were sent from.
b) The emails at the top of
your inbox should be from
the sender who is last
alphabetically.
Q3 Please see the file called
Archive1_Answer.
*A sensible name for the folder would be
a name involving the year 2012 — this
describes the contents of the folder.*

Page 45
Q1 Please see the file called
Email_Security_Answer.
Q2 The email should be addressed
to one of your contacts or
susan@cgpbooks.co.uk. The
greeting at the start of the email
should match with who your sent
the email to. Please see the file
called Sports_Club_Answer.
Q3 Please see the file called
Hotel_Booking_Answer.
*The wording of the subject and email
message might be slightly different to
the answer file. This is fine as long
as the subject is sensible (mentions a
booking) and the correct dates (in bold)
are in the message. Your email should
end with 'Yours sincerely' because you're
emailing a named person.*
Q4 Please see the file called
Washing_Machine_Answer.
*The wording of the subject and email
message might be slightly different to
the answer file. This is fine as long as
the subject is sensible and the correct
part number (in bold) is in the message.
The email should be addressed to 'Sir/
Madam'. Your email should end with
'Yours faithfully' because you're not
emailing a named person.*

Section Four — Word Processing

Page 49
Q1 Please see the file called
Typing_Answers.
Q2 Please see the file called
Amazon_Answers.
Q3 Please see the file called
Invitation1_Answers.

Page 51
Q1 Please see the file called
Invitation2_Answers.
*Your print outs should have two
invitations side by side per page.*

Page 52
Q1 Please see the file called
Gym_Answers.
*Your header boxes can be
any colour.*

Page 54
Q1 Please see the file called
Internet_Answers.
*Your print outs should look like
these pages.*
Q2 Please see the file called
Invoice_Answers.
*You should only have printed
invoices for Mrs Jones, Mrs Strauss
and Mr Butson.*

Page 59
Q1 Please see the file called
Gym_Leaflet_Answers.
*Your page doesn't have to look
exactly like this, but it should
contain these three images as they
are the most suitable ones.*
Q2 Please see the file called
Diet_Answers.
Q3 Please see the file called
Bike_Answers.
*The two most suitable images are
the bike and castle. You should
have cropped the left-hand side out
of the bike photo and rotated it so
it sits nicely. The castle should be
rotated 180° or flipped vertically.
You should have only printed page
two — the voucher.*
Q4 Please see the file called
Logo_Answer.
*Your logo doesn't need to look
exactly like this, but it should look
very similar to the sketch.*

128

Page 63

Q1 Please see the file called Poster_Answers.

Your poster doesn't need to look exactly like this, but it should:

- contain all the text from the file 'Poster',
- fit neatly onto one page,
- have a title that stands out,
- contain the 'sofa' graphic in a suitable place.

You should also have used some of the formatting techniques mentioned in part c).

Q2 Please see the file called Swimming_Answers.

Your poster doesn't need to look exactly like this, but it should:

- be A4 landscape,
- have all of the features in the correct places as shown by the plan,
- use the text and map from the file 'Swimming',
- have a suitable image inserted in the correct place — this shouldn't be watermarked and should have a credit if needed,
- use formatting features such as different font sizes and styles, colour, bolding, underlining or italics, bullet points, text alignment, etc.

You should also have corrected the spelling mistake of 'reely' in the text.

Q3 Please see the file called Pub_Answers.

Your leaflet doesn't need to look exactly like this, but it should:

- contain all of the text from page one of the file 'Pub', with any spelling mistakes corrected,
- use the first and third graphics from page two as these are the most suitable ones, placed in a suitable position,
- use one block of text from section two of page two, (see next column for more)

- use the house photo from the third section of page two as this is the most suitable, placed in a suitable position,
- use formatting features such as different font sizes and styles, colour, bolding, underlining or italics, bullet points or numbered lists, borders, text alignment, etc,
- have a nice balance of text, graphics and white space.

Section Five — Spreadsheets

Page 67
Q1 See the file called Gino_Answers.
Q2 See the file called Luxury_Answers.
Q3 See the file called Letting_Answers.
Make sure you adjust the column widths to make all the data easy to read.

Page 70
Q1 See the file called Bridgeshire_Answers.
Q2 See the file called Leekton_Answers.
The title doesn't have to look exactly like this, but it does need to have some formatting used to make it stand out, e.g. bolding, italics, coloured text or coloured background.

Page 73
Q1 See the file called Wash_Answers.
b) and c) A suitable formula for cell D2 would be =B2*C2. Then copied into cells D2 to D8.
d) A suitable formula for cell D9 would be =SUM(D2:D8).
Q2 See the file called Loan_Answers and Loan_Formula_Answers.
a) A suitable formula for cell D2 would be =B2-C2. Then copied into cells D2 to D10.
b) A suitable formula for cell B11 would be =SUM(B2:B10). Then copied into cells B11 to D11.
Abbey Little's name doesn't have to be exactly like this, but it does need to have some formatting used to make it stand out, e.g. bolding, italics, coloured text or coloured background.

Page 77
Q1 See the file called Phones_Answers.
A suitable formula for cell B16 would be =MIN(B2:B14). A suitable formula for cell B17 would be =MAX(B2:B14). A suitable formula for cell B18 would be =AVERAGE(B2:B14).
Q2 See the file called Holidays_Answers and Holidays_Formula_Answers.
a) A suitable formula for cell C4 would be =C2-B4. Then copied into cells C4 to C13.
b) A suitable formula for cell D4 would be =IF(C4>=7.5,"Yes","No"). Then copied into cells D4 to D13.

Page 79
Q1 See the file called Sales_Answers.
Q2 See the file called Interview_Answers.

Section Six — Charts and Graphs

Page 82
Q1 Please see the file called Farms_Answers.
Your labels should describe what the axes show. It's sensible to use any column titles already given. Units are needed here (tonnes).
Q2 Please see the file called Theme_Park_Answers.
Your chart may look different to this. The title and labels should describe what the chart and axes show. It's sensible to use any column titles already given. Units are needed here (thousands). You will have needed to move your chart so the data and chart could both be seen on the print out.

Page 84
Q1 Please see the file called Sales_Answers1 for the answers to a) - c) and Sales_Answers2 for the answers to d) and e).
Q2 Please see the file called Shop_Answers.
Your chart may look different to this. The title and labels should describe what the chart and axes show.

Page 86

Q1 Please see the file called Wash_ Answers1 for a) and b) and Wash_Answers2 for c) and d).

Your chart may look different to this. Any labels should describe what the data and axes show.

Q2 Please see the file called Factory_Answers.

Your chart may look different to this. The title and labels should describe what the chart and axes show.

Page 88

Q1 Please see the file called Electronics_Answers.

Your chart may look different to this. The title should describe what the chart shows. Make sure all the categories show in the legend.

Q2 Please see the file called Population_Answers1 for the answers to a) and b) and Population_Answers2 for the answers to c) and d).

Your chart may look different to this. The title and labels should describe what the chart shows.

Section Seven — Presentations

Page 89

Q1 a) Any two from, for example: text / images / video / sound / animations.

b) For example, showing the audience the information can make the talk easier to understand / it can help to make the key points stand out / it can help you remember what to say.

Pages 92-93

Q1 Please see the file called Motors_Answers.

Your print out should have two slides on each page.

Q2 Please see the file called Holiday_Answers.

Q3 Please see the file called Yourself_Answers for an example.

Your presentation doesn't have to look exactly like this, but it should:

- have four slides,
- have your name and an image on the title slide,
- have four facts about you and a suitable header on slide 2,
- have info. about where you live and a header on slide 3,
- say what your interests are and have a header on slide 4,
- have your name in a footer on every slide, and
- your print out should have two slides per page.

Page 95

Q1 Please see the file called Olympics_Answers.

Q2 Please see the file called Pyramids_Answers.

Q3 Please see the file called Technology_Answers.

Pages 98-99

Q1 Please see the file called Capitals_Answers.

Q2 Please see the file called Rome_Answers for an example.

You may have used different animations and transitions to the ones in the answer document.

Q3 Please see the file called Safari_Answers.

Q4 Please see the file called Circus_Answers for an example.

You may have used different animations and transitions to the ones in the answer document.

Page 101

Q1 Please see the file called Profit_Answers.

Your presentation doesn't need to look exactly like this, but you should have:

- increased the size of the titles on slide 2 and 3,
- moved the chart on slide 2 so it didn't overlap the text,
- corrected the spelling mistakes of 'tagret' and 'pmofit'.

Q2 Please see the file called Coffee_Answers.

Your presentation doesn't need to look exactly like this, but you should have:

- used formatting features such as different font sizes and styles,
- moved or re-sized graphics so they were appropriate and not overlapping any text,
- corrected any spelling mistakes.

Q3 Please see the file called Recruitment_Answers.

Your presentation doesn't have to look exactly like this, but it should:

- have four slides, including a title slide,
- include all the text from the file 'Recruitment_Text' in appropriate places,
- include some suitable images from the file 'Recruitment_Images' in appropriate places,
- use formatting features such as different font sizes and styles, colour, bolding, underlining or italics, bullet points, etc.

Section Eight — Databases

Page 104

Q1 Please see the file called Orders, and the table Orders.

The data types you should have are:

ID	AutoNumber
First Name	Text
Surname	Text
Amount Due	Currency
Order Date	Date/Time

Q2 Please see the file called Orders, and the table MoreOrders.

The data types you should have are:

ID	AutoNumber
First Name	Text
Surname	Text
Amount Due	Currency
Order Date	Date/Time
Paid?	Yes/No

The field 'Paid?' could have the data type of 'text', but Yes/No is far more accurate and easier to use. It sometimes appears as a tick box.

Page 106

Q1 Please see the file called Stocks_Answers.

Page 110

Q1 Please see the file called Laptops_Answers.

a) See the query Ultrawebb. You should have used the criteria **"Ultrawebb"** in the 'Manufacturer' field.

c) See the query More than 700 GB. You should have used the criteria **>700** in the 'Storage' field.

e) See the query i5. You should have used the criteria **"i5"** in the 'Processor' field, and set the sort to 'Ascending' in the 'Price' field.

g) See the reports on Laptops_Answers.

Make sure the fields are resized to fit neatly onto one page and that the reports are clear and easy to read. Totals should be removed from the price column as they aren't useful in these reports.

Q2 Please see the file called Books_Answers.

a) See the query At least £5 99. You should have used the criteria **>=5.99** and the sort 'Ascending' in the 'Price' field.

c) See the query January Releases. You should have used the criteria **Between 01/01/2014 And 31/01/2014** in the 'Release Date' field.

Your database program may automatically change this to Between #01/01/2014# And #31/01/2014#, but this is still correct.

e) See the query Surname P. You should have used the criteria **"P*"** in the 'Author Surname' field, and **>=01/02/2014** in the 'Release Date' field.

Your database program may automatically change "P*" to Like "P*", but this is still correct. The date may automatically change to #01/02/2014#. Also accept >31/01/2014 as the criteria.

g) See the reports on Books_Answers.

Make sure the fields are resized to fit neatly onto one page and that the reports are clear and easy to read. Totals should be removed from the price column as they aren't useful in these reports.

Answers — Test-style Tasks

Entry Level 3 Tasks (Pages 113-115)

Task A — Work out the cost of the prizes

Please see the file called Raffle_Prizes_Answers.

1 Work area checked and adjusted as required.
E.g. change the height or position of chair *(1 mark)*.
Computer system started correctly *(1 mark)*.
'Raffle_Prizes' file opened correctly *(1 mark)*.

2 a) Chocolate cost changed to 17 *(1 mark)*.
b) Formula added into cell B11. Either =SUM(B4:B10)
or =B4+B5+B6+B7+B8+B9+B10 *(1 mark)*.

Here you need to use a formula that works out the total cost of all the raffle prizes, so using Autosum is sensible.

3 a) Formatting of cell A6 (2 night hotel stay) changed
so that it stands out *(1 mark)*. Examples
of acceptable formatting — bolding, italics,
underlining, coloured text or box background.
b) Cells B4:B11 formatted to currency *(Maximum of 2
marks. 1 mark if not all the cells are formatted
correctly or the £ symbol has been missed or
two decimal places are not used.)*

4 Spreadsheet saved using a suitable name *(1 mark)*.
*A suitable name describes what the file contains, for
example, 'Raffle Spreadsheet' or 'Raffle Prizes Altered'.*

Task B — Design a poster to advertise the raffle

Please see the file called Raffle_Poster_Answers for
an example poster.

1 a) 'Raffle_Info' file opened correctly *(1 mark)*.
b) A poster has been created that contains: the cost of
a raffle ticket, the date the raffle is being drawn, the
prizes that can be won and where raffle tickets are
on sale *(Maximum of 4 marks, lose 1 mark for
each piece of information missed out)*.

2 'Logo_Password' file opened correctly *(1 mark)*.
'Hospice_Logo' file opened correctly *(1 mark)*.
Logo inserted into the poster *(1 mark)* in a sensible
position *(1 mark)*.
*The logo mustn't block any text or overlap the edge of the
page, and it should be fully visible when printed.*

3 A photo of a garden bench has been found using a
simple internet search *(1 mark)*. Photo inserted into
the poster *(1 mark)* in a sensible position *(1 mark)*.
*Any photo of a garden bench is suitable. The photo
mustn't block any text or overlap the edge of the page,
and it should be fully visible when printed.*

4 a) The poster has been formatted using features such
as: font sizes, font styles, colour, underlining, bold
or italics, alignment, bullet points, page borders.
(1 mark for each different feature up to 4 marks)
b) The poster should contain accurate information that
matches that in the file 'Raffle_Info' *(1 mark)*.
A spell check should have been run to identify and
correct any spelling errors *(1 mark)*.

5 The poster has been saved using a suitable name
(1 mark) and printed out *(1 mark)*.
*A suitable name describes what the file contains, for
example, 'Raffle Poster.'*

Task C — Send an email message

Please see the file called Email_Answers for
example emails.

1 'Email' file opened correctly *(1 mark)*.

2 The email is addressed to
susan@cgpbooks.co.uk *(1 mark)*. A sensible
subject line is used *(1 mark)*. The email starts and
ends appropriately *(1 mark)*.
Question 1 answer: £654 *(1 mark)*.
*If you got the total cost of the raffle prizes wrong in
Task A and used that cost here you'll still get the mark.*

Question 2 answer: Any two sensible answers from
information listed on page 22. For example, adjust
the height of your chair so that you're at the correct
height for using the keyboard comfortably OR adjust
your chair so your feet are resting on the floor OR
adjust your seating arrangements so you don't have
to stretch for things like the mouse OR adjust your
screen to a comfortable height *(1 mark for each
suggestion up to 2 marks)*.
Question 3 answer: E.g. to stop viruses from
damaging your computer OR to stop viruses from
slowing your computer down OR to stop viruses from
stealing information from your computer *(1 mark for
any sensible suggestion)*.

3 Email checked for errors (e.g. by running a spell
check) *(1 mark)*. Email printed out *(1 mark)*.

4 Computer system shutdown correctly *(1 mark)*.

Level 1 Tasks (Pages 116-120)
Part A
Task 1 — Eccle Riggs Hall

Please see the file called
Evidence_Doc_L1_Answers.
In the file 'Evidence_Doc_L1' you should have:
A screen shot of the search and results *(1 mark)*.
Keywords must be visible and include Eccle Riggs
and address *(1 mark)*.
The address: Eccle Riggs Hall, Broughton-in-
Furness, Cumbria, LA20 6BN *(1 mark)*.
URL given for the website where the address was
found *(1 mark)*.
*It's really important that your screen shot is large
enough for the assessor to read your keywords.*

Part B
Task 2 — Costs of the party

Please see the files called Party_Costs_Answers
and Party_Costs_Formulas_Answers.
a) 'Party_Costs' file opened correctly *(1 mark)*.
Formula to work out total cost of drinks added into
cell D4: =B4*C4 *(1 mark)*.

Formula to work out total cost of transport added into cell D5: =B5*C5 *(1 mark)*.

Here the formulas needed to multiply the cost per person by the number of people to give the total cost.

Formula for total cost of party added into cell D11. Either =SUM(D4:D9) or =D4+D5+D6+D7+D8+D9 *(1 mark)*.

b) All of the costs in column D formatted to currency with a £ symbol and two decimal places *(1 mark)*. Widths of all columns adjusted to see all the data in them *(1 mark)*. Formatting of the spreadsheet in at least one way, for example borders added, column headings highlighted somehow, total cost of the party highlighted somehow *(1 mark)*.

When you're asked to format a spreadsheet think currency, width and highlighting (e.g. bold and colour).

c) Spreadsheet printed with formulas shown *(1 mark)*.

Task 3 — Party food

Please see the file called Food_Suppliers_Answers.

a) 'Food_Suppliers' file opened correctly *(1 mark)*. Data altered to ascending order by numbers in column D *(1 mark)*. Data in columns A and D (Supplier and Total) used to make a column (bar) chart *(1 mark)*.

A line graph is OK but it's not the most sensible one here. A pie chart or scatter graph isn't suitable.

The chart must have a suitable title mentioning 'suppliers' and 'total cost' or 'quote' *(1 mark)*. X-axis must have a suitable label *(1 mark)*. Y-axis must have a suitable label *(1 mark)*. Chart legend deleted *(1 mark)*.

The legend is made automatically, but it isn't needed when there's only one set of data like here.

The chart makes sense and there are no unnecessary data or spelling mistakes *(1 mark)*. The chart is printed on a separate sheet in landscape orientation *(1 mark)*.

Please see the files called Task 3 chart and Evidence_Doc_L1_Answers.

b) A word processing file called 'Task 3 chart' should be saved somewhere sensible *(1 mark)*. The file called 'Task 3 chart' should contain a copy of the chart created in part a) *(1 mark)*. In the file 'Evidence_Doc_L1' you should have a screen shot to show that the file 'Task 3 chart' is a read-only file *(1 mark)*.

Task 4 — Poster to advertise the party

Please see the file called Party_Poster_Answer for an example poster.

a) Suitable program used to create poster. For example, Microsoft®Word® or Publisher® *(1 mark)*. Details of the party from the file 'Party_Details' included in the poster *(1 mark)*. Address from Part A Task 1 included *(1 mark)*.

If you got the address wrong in Task 1, but used that address here you'll still get the mark here.

Two suitable graphics from 'Party_Graphics' inserted into the poster (not the lily or stone heads) *(1 mark)*, in a suitable position and size *(1 mark)*. Logo has been inserted into the poster *(1 mark)* in a sensible position *(1 mark)*.

The logo and graphics mustn't block any text or overlap the edge of the page, and they should be large enough to print nicely.

Poster fits onto one A4 page *(1 mark)*. Font size and style appropriate for a poster (e.g. point 16 at least) *(1 mark)*. Formatting used to attract attention, for example: title in large font, different font sizes and styles used, colour, underlining, bold or italics, different alignments, bullet points, page borders *(1 mark for each different feature used, up to 3 marks)*. A spell check should have been run to identify and correct any spelling errors *(1 mark)*.

b) The poster should have been saved with a suitable name *(1 mark)*. The poster printed out A4 portrait *(1 mark)*.

Task 5 — Presentation to senior managers

Please see the file called Food_Presentation_Answer for an example presentation.

a) Suitable program used to create the presentation For example, Microsoft®PowerPoint® *(1 mark)*. The presentation contains three slides (as described in the task) *(1 mark)*. The first slide (title slide) contains the title Christmas Party *(1 mark)* and a suitable image from the file 'Party_Graphics' (not the lily or stone heads). *(1 mark)*. Logo has been inserted into each slide *(1 mark)*. Logo and graphic are inserted in a sensible position *(1 mark)*.

The logo and graphic mustn't block any text or overlap the edge of the slides and they should be a suitable size.

One slide contains the chart from Task 3 *(1 mark)*. One slide contains information from 'Food_Details' *(1 mark)*. A suitable font style and size used for title slide *(1 mark)*. Non-title slides should have suitable titles that describe the content *(1 mark)*. A spell check should have been run to identify and correct any spelling errors *(1 mark)*. The presentation has a consistent format throughout *(1 mark)*.

This means the same fonts, similar font sizes, same backgrounds (if any have been used) and there's a consistent look throughout the presentation.

b) The presentation should have been saved with a suitable name *(1 mark)*.

For example, 'Christmas Party Presentation'.

The slides should have been printed out with two slides per page *(1 mark)*.

Task 6 — Transport Arrangements

Please see the file called
Evidence_Doc_L1_Answers.
a) A screen shot shows all records and:
   Check-box in the 'Need Transport?' field unchecked
   in Matthew Scott's record *(1 mark)*.
   Becky Potter's record (ID 15) deleted *(1 mark)*.
   New record added with correct data in the following
   fields:

First Name	John
Surname	Williams
Town	Broughton
Need Transport?	Checked

   (2 marks for all correct, 1 mark for 3 correct.)
b) Printed report fits onto one A4 page *(1 mark)*.
   Report shows 'First Name', 'Surname' and
   'Town' only *(1 mark)*. Report only contains the 14
   records with a check in the 'Need Transport?' field
   (1 mark). Records sorted alphabetically by town
   (1 mark).

Task 7 — Email your poster

Please see the file called
Evidence_Doc_L1_Answers.
Email addressed to tom@cgpbooks.co.uk *(1 mark)*.
A sensible subject line is used (including the word
'poster') *(1 mark)*. The poster file is attached to
the email *(1 mark)*. The email message contains a
question asking if the poster is suitable *(1 mark)*.
The email starts and ends appropriately and has a
suitable business tone *(1 mark)*.
A suitably-sized screen shot of the email has been
added to the file 'Evidence_Doc_L1' *(1 mark)*.

Task 8 — Organise your work

Please see the file called
Evidence_Doc_L1_Answers.
Different folders created to store work files *(1 mark)*
with suitable names *(1 mark)*.
*Suitable names should describe the contents of the folder,
for example, 'Party Poster Files' or 'Task 4_Party Poster.*

A suitably-sized screen shot of the folders has been
added to the file 'Evidence_Doc_L1' *(1 mark)*.

Task 9 — Questions

a) The file could be password-protected *(1 mark)*.
b) www.bbc.co.uk/news *(1 mark)*.
*Web addresses (URLs) start with www or http or https.
Email addresses usually have an @ in them. .jpeg and
.html are file extensions for a graphic and a web page.*

Level 2 Tasks (Pages 121-125)
Part A
Task 1 — Travelling to the show

Please see the file called
Evidence_Doc_L2_Answers.
In the file 'Evidence_Doc_L2' you should have:
A screen shot of the internet search engine keywords
and results *(1 mark)* and screen shot(s) of a page

showing the price of the return ticket *(1 mark)*.
Suitable keywords used *(1 mark)* including
advanced search notation (*, ", OR or AND)
(1 mark).
URL given for the website where the ticket price was
found *(1 mark)*. A screen shot of the bookmarked
page showing the ticket price *(1 mark)*.

Task 2 — Email about train tickets

Please see the file called
Evidence_Doc_L2_Answers.
Email addressed to a.harrop@gmx.co.uk *(1 mark)*.
A sensible subject line is used (e.g. uses the words
train tickets, prices, show) *(1 mark)*. The URL of the
ticket web page and a price is in the email *(1 mark)*.
*The URL doesn't need to be a link, and the price can be
different to the one given here.*

The email starts and ends appropriately and has a
suitable business tone *(1 mark)*.
*Emails should always have a suitable subject line and
start and end with greetings like Dear and Best wishes.*

A suitably sized screen shot of the email has been
added to the file 'Evidence_Doc_L2' *(1 mark)*.
A suitably sized screen shot of the contact details
given for Amanda added to the file 'Evidence_Doc_
L2' *(1 mark)*. The contact details match those given
in the file 'Amanda_Harrop' sowing the file has been
opened correctly *(1 mark)*.

Part B
Task 3 — Meeting buyers at the show

Please see the files called Buyer_Data_Answers and
Buyer_Data_Formula_Answers.
a) 'Buyer_Data' file opened correctly *(1 mark)*.
   Formula for total value added into cell H2. Either
   =SUM(B2:G2) or =B2+C2+D2+E2+F2+G2
   (1 mark). Correct formula also in cells H3 to H8
   (1 mark).
   All of the values in column B-H formatted to
   currency with a £ symbol and two decimal places
   (1 mark). Widths of all columns adjusted to see
   all the data in them *(1 mark)*. Formatting of the
   spreadsheet in at least one way, for example
   borders added, column headings highlighted
   somehow, buyers to invite highlighted somehow
   (1 mark).
   *When you're asked to format a spreadsheet think
   currency, width and highlighting (e.g. bold and colour).*
b) IF formula entered in cells I2 to I8:
   =IF(H2>=25000,"Invite","Don't Invite") *(1 mark)*.
   Correct cell selected in IF function (total order
   amount — H2) *(1 mark)*. Correct use of greater
   than or equals symbol *(1 mark)*. Correct value
   of 25000 *(1 mark)*. Correct words appearing
   when IF function is true and false *(1 mark)*.
   Invite showing in column I for Samuels, Drinks
   Wholesale, United Drinks Distribution and
   Cheesemans *(1 mark)*. Spreadsheet printed with
   all data clearly showing *(1 mark)*. Spreadsheet
   printed with all formulas clearly showing *(1 mark)*.

Task 4 — Invitation to buyers

Please see the files called Letter_Field_Answers and Letter_Final_Answers.

'Letter' file opened correctly *(1 mark)*. 'Logo' file opened correctly *(1 mark)* and logo inserted into a suitable position in the letter *(1 mark)*. The date added to the letter in a suitable position *(1 mark)*. A spell check should have been run to identify and correct any spelling errors *(1 mark)*.

File 'Buyer_Details' opened correctly and used to supply data for mail merge *(1 mark)*.

Correct merge fields added to letter in the correct places *(3 marks for all correct, 2 mark for 8 correct, 1 mark for 5 correct)*.

Letter printed showing merged field names *(1 mark)*.

Letters correctly merged and printed out to buyers that are being invited to the show only — Samuels, Drinks Wholesale, United Drinks Distribution and Cheesemans *(2 marks for all correct letters, 1 mark if 2 correct. Allow follow through of any incorrect buyers from Task 3)*.

Task 5 — Costs and benefits of attending the show

Please see the file called Costs_And_Orders_Answers.

'Costs_And_Orders' file opened correctly *(1 mark)*. Bar/column chart or line graph produced with two bars (or two lines) for each year *(1 mark)*. All data given used in the chart *(1 mark)*. Appropriate title for chart that contains mention of costs and orders and that it shows data for 5 years *(1 mark)*. Appropriate axis labels used *(1 mark)*. Legend is used *(1 mark)* and labels are correctly spelt *(1 mark)*.

Task 6 — Presentation for the sales team

Please see the files called Evidence_Doc_L2 and Show_Presentation_Answer for an example presentation.

a) Suitable program used to create the presentation. For example, Microsoft®PowerPoint® *(1 mark)*. The presentation contains a title slide with a suitable header *(1 mark)* and company logo *(1 mark)*.

A suitable header could mention the following: 'Food and Drink Show', 'Birmingham' or 'NEC'.

A slide containing accurate schedule information from the file 'Schedule_And_Aims' *(1 mark)*. A slide containing accurate aims for the day imported from the file 'Schedule_And_Aims' *(1 mark)*. Aim 5 should have had figure of £9 900 added into brackets (from Task 5) *(1 mark)*. A slide containing the chart from Task 5 correctly inserted in a sensible place *(1 mark)*. Graphics used are in suitable locations on all the slides (e.g. not in way of other text) *(1 mark)*. All slides (except title slide) have the company logo present at a suitable size in the top right of the slide *(1 mark)*.

The logo on title slide should be larger than the logos on each of the other slides in the presentation.

All slides (except title slide) have a footer *(1 mark)* that says 'Wholesome Drinks' *(1 mark)*. There is evidence of a slide transition set being used *(1 mark)*. A suitable font style and size used for title slide *(1 mark)*. Non-title slides should have suitable titles that describe the content *(1 mark)*. A spell check should have been run to identify and correct any spelling errors *(1 mark)*. The presentation has a consistent format *(1 mark)*.

This means the same fonts, similar font sizes, same backgrounds (if any have been used) and there's a consistent look throughout the presentation.

In the file 'Evidence_Doc_L2' you should have a screen shot showing a slide transition *(1 mark)*. The slides should have been printed out with two slides per page *(1 mark)*.

b) A folder created *(1 mark)* and sensibly named to describe what is in it including the presentation *(1 mark)*. A compressed (zipped) folder also created *(1 mark)*. In the file 'Evidence_Doc_L2' you should have a screen shot showing the contents of the folder *(1 mark)* and a compressed folder with a similar name *(1 mark)*.

Task 7 — Organising meetings

Please see the file called Evidence_Doc_L2_Answers.

a) A screen shot shows field names imported into table with no errors *(1 mark)*. The screen shot shows data imported into table with no errors *(1 mark)*. A screen shot shows a unique identifier (ID) has been assigned *(1 mark)*. The screen shot shows that the 'Date' field has been set to 'Date/Time' *(1 mark)* and all other imported fields set to 'Text' *(1 mark)*.

b) A screen shot shows #02/09/2014# as the criteria for 'Date' *(1 mark)*. The screen shot shows either "Lunchtime" Or "Afternoon", or Not "Morning", as the criteria for 'Meeting Slot' *(2 marks for criteria met correctly, 1 mark if criteria returns only one of either "Lunchtime" or "Afternoon")*. The printed report fits onto one page, and is easy to read *(1 mark)*. The printed report shows 'Company' and 'Meeting Slot' fields only *(1 mark)*. The printed report shows the correct 7 records, for the following companies: Samuels, Drinks Wholesale, Slurpers, Great British Drink Co., HWPD, Sapor and Juice Distributors *(1 mark)*.

Task 8 — Questions

a) Any keyboard shortcut *(1 mark)* and correct explanation *(1 mark)*. See page 16 for sensible suggestions.

b) To reduce the size of the email / to reduce the time it takes to send the email *(1 mark)*.

Glossary

A

Address bar

The bar in a browser window where you enter web addresses or URLs.

Alignment

A way of formatting text so it lies to the left-hand side of a page, to the right-hand side, is justified or is centred in the middle of a page.

Antivirus software

A program used to protect a computer from viruses.

Application software

The programs on a computer, like word processors, email and database programs.

Attachment

A file that is sent with an email. For example, graphics can be sent as email attachments.

Axis

A line along the bottom and up the left-hand side of most graphs and charts.

B

Bar chart

A chart which shows information using bars of different heights.

Bcc

A way of sending a copy of an email to someone privately. Only the sender of the email can see who an email has been Bcc'd to.

Blog

A website where people can write their opinions for others to read. Blog is short for 'web log'.

Bold text

Text with thick lines, like this: **bold**.

Bookmark

A link to a website, stored on your computer for easy access.

Border

The outline given to something, like a cell or document, to make it stand out.

Browser

Software used to access web pages and the internet.

C

Cc

A way of sending a copy of an email to someone. Everyone that receives the email can see who the email has been Cc'd to.

Cell

A rectangular box in a spreadsheet where one piece of data can be stored.

Cell reference

A letter and number which describes where a cell is in a spreadsheet. The letter describes the column, the number describes the row.

Click

In this book, this means click on something with the left mouse button.

Clip art

A ready-made image gallery found in some programs, like Word®, or on the internet.

Column chart

See 'Bar chart'.

Compressed file or folder

A file or folder that has been compressed (zipped) to reduce its size.

Control panel

An area of your computer where you can change settings like screen resolution and icon size.

Cropping

Cutting the edges off a graphic.

Cursor

A flashing black bar showing where text will be entered.

Database

An organised collection of data.

Desktop

The screen you usually see after you log in to a computer.

Double-click

In this book, this means click twice very quickly on the left mouse button.

Email

An electronic message.

Favourite

See 'Bookmark'.

Field

A category of data in a database.

Filtering data

Hiding data so that only data that matches certain criteria (rules) can be seen.

Font

The style of text, like this: Times New Roman.

Footer

Text that appears at the bottom of every page when it's printed out. For example, a title, date or your name.

Formula bar

The bar in a spreadsheet where you see, enter or edit the data in a cell.

Forwarding

Sending on an email that you have received to someone else.

Function

A formula which comes already set up in a spreadsheet program.

Group distribution list

A list of email addresses saved as a group.

Hardware

The physical parts of a computer, like the monitor, keyboard and hard drive.

Header

Text that appears at the top of every page when it's printed out. For example, a title, date or your name.

Home page

The web page which opens when you click on a browser.

Icons

Small pictures that can be clicked on to open a file or program.

Importing data

Bringing data from one file into a different file. For example, you can import data from a text file into a spreadsheet file.

Inbox

The folder where emails that are sent to an email address are stored.

Input device

Hardware that's used to enter data into a computer. For example, a keyboard.

Internet

A worldwide network of computers all linked together.

Italic text

Text that slopes to the right, like this: *italic*.

Keywords

Important words typed into the search bar of an internet search engine.

Legend

A list which shows what data is plotted on a chart or graph.

Line graph

A graph which shows data using a line.

Link

An image or piece of text which takes you to a web page when you click on it.

Mail merge

A word processing function that's used to create multiple documents where only a few details change each time.

Margin

The gap without text found at the top, bottom and sides of a document.

Master slide

A template for slides in a presentation.

Operating system

The software that controls the whole computer and runs the application software.

Orientation

The direction in which a document is displayed or printed. There are two orientations — portrait (vertical) and landscape (horizontal).

Output device

Hardware that uses the data from a computer.

Pie chart

A chart which shows data using slices of a complete circle.

Presentation software

Software used to make slides.

Primary key

A 'unique identifier' — a field in a database containing data that is different for each record, such as an ID number.

Program

See 'Application software'.

Query

A method of finding data in database tables by using a set of rules.

Recipient

Someone who receives something. For example, the recipient of an email is the person who receives it (the person it's sent to).

Record

A row of data in a database table.

Report

A way of presenting formatted data in databases.

Right-click

In this book, this means click on something with the right mouse button.

Scattergraph

A special kind of line graph which is used when all the data you need to plot is numbers.

Screen shot

An image of what is currently showing on the screen. Also called a screen print, screen dump or screen capture.

Search engine

A website that searches lots of other websites for keywords typed into its search bar.

Slide

A page used in presentation software. They're made into a slide show and shown during presentations or talks.

Slide show

An option in presentation software that lets you move through slides one by one. For example, during a presentation or talk.

Social media

Websites which allow people to stay in touch with lots of other people.

Software

See 'Application software'.

Sorting data

Arranging data into a certain order.
For example, alphabetically (A-Z).

Spam

Emails that you receive that aren't from people you know and that you haven't asked for.

Spreadsheet software

Software which stores data in cells that are organised in rows and columns. Spreadsheet programs can also carry out calculations with the data.

Start button

Used to open the Start Menu. Often found in the bottom left of a desktop.

Tab (on a toolbar)

A type of button found at the top of some software screens that opens different toolbars when clicked.

Taskbar

The row of buttons usually found at the bottom of the desktop.

Text wrapping

The way text is organised around a graphic or shape in some documents.

Toolbar

A row of useful buttons found at the top of some software windows.

Transition

An effect you can add to slides in presentations. Transitions are how new slides appear during the slide show. For example, flying in, or fading in.

Troll

Someone who uses the internet to upset or harass others.

Unique Identifier

A field in a database which is different for every record, such as an ID number.

URL

The address of a web page or website.
Also called a web address.

Validation rule

A rule that stops certain data from being entered into a database table. Often used to prevent mistakes. For example, allowing only 'yes' or 'no' in a field.

Virus

A harmful program made to infect computers. They can make things stop working, make the computer run slower or steal information from the computer.

Web browser

See 'Browser'.

Web page

A document located on the internet.

Website

Lots of web pages linked together.

Wildcard

A symbol used in searches that can stand for any character or characters.

Word processor

Software that lets you edit and format text and graphics. It can be used to create letters, posters, leaflets, articles, newsletters, invoices, etc.

Zipped (compressed) file or folder

See 'Compressed file or folder'.

Index

O

Office® 2010 1
Office® features 14
operating systems 9
operators
  in databases 108
  in spreadsheets 76, 77
  internet use 29
orientation 50
output devices 6

P

page borders 51
page numbers 50
passwords 7, 18
paste 15
PCs 3
pen drives 17
pie charts 87
pointers 5
presentations 89
primary keys 103
printing 15
  charts and graphs 82
  databases 109
  presentations 92
  spreadsheets 70
  word processing files 51
programs (software) 9

Q

queries 107

R

read-only files and folders 18
records 102
relative cell references 17
removable storage devices 17
reports 109
resizing graphics 55
right-clicking 5
rotating graphics 55

S

safely removing devices 17
save as 18
saving files 18
scattergraphs 86
screen shots (screen dumps, prints or captures) 24
search engines 26
searching
  databases 107
  for emails 41
  on your computer 12
  using the Find feature 14
settings (changing them) 21
shortcuts 16
shutting down a computer 4
sitting properly at a computer 22
slides 90
slide shows 92
slide transitions 97
smartphones 3
software (programs) 9
sorting
  in databases 105
  emails 41
  in spreadsheets 78
spellchecking 48
spreadsheets 64
start menu 4
starting up 4

T

tabs 13
tables
  in databases 102
  in presentations 96
  in word processing files 52
tablets 3
taskbar 11
text alignment 47
text wrapping 56
toolbars 13
transitions 97

U

undo 15
unique identifiers 102
USB memory sticks 17
user interfaces 11

V

validation rules 103
viruses 43

W

web pages (websites) 25
wildcards 29, 72, 108
windows 11-13
Windows® 7 1
word processing 46

Z

zipped (compressed) files and folders 20